# HOW
## TO
# MAKE
## IT
## IN AMERICA

An Immigrant's Path to Purpose,
Patriotism, and Life Well Lived

**Paul Moody Tsou, MD**

THE
SELF
PUBLISHING
AGENCY

Paul Tsou
How To Make It In America
An Immigrant's Path to Purpose, Patriotism, and Life Well Lived

SHC Enterprises
Copyright © 2025 by Paul Tsou
First Edition

Softcover ISBN 979-8-9998082-1-9
Hardcover ISBN 979-8-9998082-0-2
eBook ISBN  979-8-9998082-2-6

Book Design | Ashley Russell Designs
Editor | Licia Morelli
Publishing Management | TSPA The Self Publishing Agency, Inc.

My adoptive parents, Mami Ai-Ling Tsou and Daddy, Dr. Szu-Tai Tsou, were the kindest, most loving, forgiving, and understanding of the son's ways. In that environment, I was free to explore my curiosities. My autobiography shows the results: A good education, a never-boring profession continued into my old age, a stable family, and good health both in mind and body.

Schumarry by herself gave me life essential elements for a stable family life and good health both in mind and body in our marriage, still going strong after fifty four years.

—Paul Moody Tsou

# Foreword

## By Schumarry Chao

Paul possesses a strong sense of self. He lives with quiet integrity, naturally honoring his values without needing to force or overthink them. He is a man of few, but precise, words. He speaks with economy, delivering the essence of his thoughts in just a handful of well-chosen phrases. You'll never be confused about what he means. His clarity comes from both training and temperament, shaped by years as an orthopaedic surgeon, a military officer, and a child raised in the lean decade during and following World War II. Growing up in his household, resources were few. A child might have one pair of shoes, worn until the soles peeled away. Allowances didn't exist. Money was given only for necessity, and rewards came only when something truly worthwhile had been earned. Even then, they were offered with love and a quiet sense of purpose.

My own upbringing was quite the opposite. I loved my family by giving generously, not waiting for a special occasion or milestone. In Paul's family, subtle encouragement was ever present. In mine, it was loud and clear. Maybe that's why our individual strong or weak personality traits found the perfect fit in one another.

Before we met at Queen's Hospital in Honolulu, Paul was a mystery to me, and I was equally unknown to him. He never asked about me, never pried. We exchanged a brief glance while waiting for the elevator. I noticed his white, house staff jacket with the University of California San Francisco patch on the sleeve. I wondered what kind of surgical resident came to Hawaii for training, especially since the Hawaii Medical School had just opened its doors. Hawaii, lovely as it is, isn't exactly a global capital of academic medicine.

But Paul was not like others. He didn't advertise himself. He didn't offer a long résumé, nor did he seem to be auditioning for any role in life. I, on the other hand, had pages of experience and accolades to my name. He seemed content with who he was, unimpressed by social hierarchies or superficial charm. He didn't compete for attention, and that intrigued me. His quiet confidence filled in something I didn't even know I was missing.

It was Dr. Glauber Liese, the Chair of Radiology at Queen's, who finally introduced us, two people from the same San Francisco training program who had never met until we were 2,500 miles from home. Call it coincidence. I call it fate.

Paul was already well-traveled and seasoned by the time we met, a third-year orthopaedic chief resident, with military service on two Coast Guard vessels during the Vietnam War, and a deep love for art, music, and global history. I saw in him not only intellect and steadiness, but a worldview shaped by challenge and perspective. Within a four month period, we strolled the path of love, engagement, and marriage at Stanford Memorial Church. Both sets of parents were present, along with our friends and medical colleagues. Fifty years later, we returned to that same church to celebrate half a century of life and love, this time with grown children and many of the same people who had stood with us at the beginning.

Paul's quiet strength, his steadiness, and his complete comfort in his own skin were essential to my own success. In the 1970s and 80s, women pursuing demanding careers, especially doctor wives, were often seen as unusual, even inappropriate. At medical conferences, I was told more than once, "Don't worry, honey, your husband will be successful soon, and then you won't have to work anymore." Many of Paul's peers assumed my work, and my frequent career changes, reflected poorly on him. But Paul never flinched. He never tried to diminish me, compete with me, or feel threatened by what others thought. He simply supported me. I never had to worry about his trust, his pride, or his presence. Whether I was home or away, on stage or at the back of the room, Paul remained constant, grounded, encouraging, and unbothered by whose spotlight we were standing in. For that, and for so much more, I am deeply grateful.

As I write this, I am seventy-eight years old. Paul is eighty-three. We still enjoy each other's company, walk or use the treadmill three to five miles a day, and keep our minds in crisp clarity. We live in Las Vegas, Nevada. Of course, time has made its quiet claims on our bodies. But we're fortunate, what needs mending can be restored through medicine, and what needs support, we find in each other.

This book is a story of resilience, partnership, and the enduring joy of discovery, not just of the world, but of one another. I hope our journey offers you insight, laughter, and, above all, a sense of possibility at every stage of life.

—Schumarry Chao

# Introduction

This is the autobiography of an American orthopaedic spine surgeon, ethnically Chinese, who was orphaned before the age of four during the height of the Sino-Japanese War in World War II. Now, at eighty-four, he reflects on his life, his journey, and what it has meant to be an American.

By the standards of his family, friends, and peers, he has "made it." But in retirement, with time to look back, he sets his own standards, examining his life as a whole, then breaking it down into five distinct sections. In doing so, he finds not just success, but a deep and abiding sense of fulfillment.

# Clarification on the Author's Given Names

Clarification is in order on the author's given name, Moody, subordinated by the name Paul at the age of 12, as this is the first important transition point in the boy's life. "Moody" was given to him as an infant, when he was just one or two years old, by his biological grandfather, a Methodist elder. The name was inspired by the 19th-century American Methodist evangelist, Dwight L. Moody. To this day, close maternal family members still call him by that name, and it remains his middle name on all legal documents.

However, "Paul" was not part of his original name. It was given to him at the suggestion of a minister after he and his mother arrived in the United States. In their first year in America, they lived in Coaldale, Pennsylvania, and attended a Presbyterian church five miles away from Coaldale in the town of Tamaqua. The church's pastor, a former missionary to China before the Communist takeover in 1949, advised that Moody should have a more familiar first name, one that Americans would recognize easily. And so, "Paul" was added. From that point forward, his full legal name became **Paul Moody Tsou**.

# Part One:

From Orphan to Medical School Graduate

# 1

From birth to age four, Moody lived in a small, quiet world just steps away from the chaos of World War II's intense military activity on land and in the air. The time and place were Chungking, China. Moody's story begins on his birthday, November 12, 1941, twenty-five days before the Pearl Harbor attack, and the Sino-Japanese War had already been waged for ten years. His earliest memories date back to when he was about three years old.

During the war, his family consisted only of him and his mother. No other relatives were present, and what happened to them remains unknown. His mother worked as a surgical nurse in a wartime hospital located just beyond a small hill outside the city of Chungking. The hospital compound was separated from the staff residence by nothing more than a low-lying rice paddy. While his mother worked her shifts, Moody was left alone in the residence, unattended.

One afternoon, Moody accompanied his mother and several hospital staff members to a festival celebration on the banks of the Yangtze River. Near the festival grounds, his mother pointed out a building, the live-in nursery and children's dormitory. She explained that soon, on the days she worked, he would stay there. Moody didn't fully grasp what that meant.

Then the day arrived. Hand in hand, he and his mother walked to the dormitory. The reality of what was happening didn't sink in until she said, "Goodbye, be a good boy. I will come back in a few days to take you home for the weekend." Then, she stepped out through the gate.

Tears poured down Moody's face, turning into uncontrollable sobs. He was placed in a dormitory bed, still crying. By morning, all was quiet, but Moody was nowhere to be found.

Later that same morning, the dormitory supervisor called his mother. The boy had gone missing. Fortunately, he was found in the hospital waiting area, having made his way there on his own. When his mother saw him, she hugged him tightly. There was no punishment, only a promise.

"You need to return to the dormitory tomorrow," she told him. "You will stay there until I come to bring you home."

And so, the arrangement continued, uninterrupted, until the end of the war.

How did a three-year-old boy manage to crawl under a fence and walk nearly two miles alone in the dark to find his way back to his mother? The answer remains a mystery.

As long as Moody has lived, he has had no information about his biological father or his two older brothers. The little he did come to know was not shared with him until years later, when he and his adoptive mother, Ai-Ling, immigrated to Hong Kong in 1948. His adoptive father, Stephen, later voyaged to the United States.

# 2

On September 2, 1945, Japan's unconditional surrender marked the end of World War II. With the war over, resettlement orders arrived for the hospital units. Most of the hospital staff had survived the war's evacuations and continued working in the nearest unoccupied territories. Now, it was time for those from more distant regions to be reassigned.

Moody's mother had originally worked at a hospital in Nanking, but the facility had been destroyed during the Japanese assault on the city in 1938. Her new assignment placed her in Jianjiung, a provincial town along the Yangtze River, about 100 miles downstream from Nanking. Jianjiung was well known for its aromatic dark vinegar and pork dishes, but life there was anything but comfortable.

Mother and Moody traveled down the Yangtze by river transport boat, first stopping in Nanking before continuing by bus to Jianjiung. Upon arrival, they found themselves in a town ill-equipped for resettlement. The river docks were inadequate due to the season's low water levels, and housing for hospital staff was sparse, no furniture, no beds, just straw for mattresses. But they made do.

For Moody, the most significant challenge was the absence of schooling and adult supervision. With no formal education available and no playmates his age, he spent his days in the fields, catching birds and squirrels.

Then, a new possibility emerged.

# 3

Throughout the war, Moody's mother had exchanged small talk with a fellow surgeon. Now, with peace restored, their conversations turned to something more serious—marriage. But Moody presented a complication. His presence could slow the pace of their relationship. Was there a solution for his future?

An answer arrived in the form of an old friendship.

Moody's mother had a childhood friend and former nursing school classmate, Tsou Ai-Ling, whom Moody would come to call "Mami." Ai-Ling and her husband, Stephen Tsou, had been married for nearly a decade but were unable to have children due to medical reasons. Stephen, a graduate of St. John's Medical School in Shanghai, had just been appointed Superintendent of Szuchow County Public Hospital. The couple had survived the war, escaping the devastation of Nanking and serving in a reorganized medical unit stationed on the Burma Road. Now, with the war behind them, they were ready to settle down, and they longed for a child.

Letters were exchanged between Moody's mother and Mami. Adoption was raised as a real possibility. But before any decision could be made, several critical questions had to be answered:

- *Would Moody be willing to leave his mother?*
- *Would he adapt and be welcomed into the old-fashioned Tsou family?*
- *Would his maternal grandfather be willing to part with his only living grandson?*
- *Would the prospective parents accept Moody's unusual, curious behavior and tendencies?*

There were two concerns regarding Moody's health. First, he had a nickel-sized, 3mm deep scar on his right buttock, a lasting imprint from a childhood medical incident. When he was an infant, a syringe needle had accidentally lodged too deeply, breaking off and requiring exploratory extraction, which left a permanent indentation. Second, Moody had a tendency to wander. He was highly energetic and had a habit of exploring unfamiliar places. His new parents would need to keep a close eye on him, especially when traveling.

Despite these concerns, the Tsous were eager to proceed. But before making it official, a trial visit was arranged.

# 4

Mami and Daddy (as Moody would later call them) traveled to Jianjiuang to pick him up. Together, they boarded a train to Szuchow, where Moody would stay with them for a week.

The trial visit went smoothly. Moody showed no resistance, even expressing his willingness to stay with his new guardians for a few days. He quickly took to the new environment, playing with a distant relative's child. When the trial visit ended, he returned to Jianjiuang, and the decision was made: He would become part of the Tsou family.

Moody and his mother then traveled to Nanking to visit his maternal grandparents. His grandfather, despite his deep love for the boy, ultimately gave his blessing. He took comfort in knowing that his grandson would be raised in a Christian home.

The adoption process required no legal documentation, only a verbal agreement. With that, Moody's mother relinquished her responsibility, believing she had secured a brighter future for Moody. Free from the burden of single parenthood, she felt ready to remarry and, perhaps, have more children of her own.

Moody's formative years were under the care of Ai-Ling and Stephen Tsou. Ai-Ling (later anglicized to Eileen) and Stephen were well-educated medical professionals, and their economic standing placed them in China's upper-middle class, a rare privilege in a country still recovering from years of war.

Moody spent about twenty months in Szuchow and Shanghai, where the Tsous had deep roots. Life in Szuchow followed traditional Chinese customs, and the food was exquisite. Daddy, a true connoisseur of food, ensured that meals reflected the rich culinary traditions of Jiangsu province.

It was a time of freedom and discovery. Moody roamed within the hospital compound, nurtured by attentive and loving parents. But the rules were firm. He was taught to respect elders, to listen when spoken to, to practice absolute honesty, and to ask permission when necessary. These principles, instilled in childhood, would later echo through the institutions and organizations he encountered in adulthood.

In 1947, Stephen Tsou earned a government two-year fellowship to study public health in America. He intended to utilize this opportunity as soon as his Visa was granted by the US. His visa application was successful.

In the final months before leaving China, Moody lived in Shanghai with his paternal grandfather, waiting for the next chapter of his life to unfold.

The journey ahead was clear. Mami and Moody would travel to Hong Kong aboard the SS President Cleveland, a repurposed troop ship. From there, the same vessel would carry Daddy across the Pacific to America.

In Shanghai, Moody's grandfather lived in a townhouse on East Nanking Road. The residence shared walls with neighboring homes, and its front door opened into a wide communal alleyway. Since few families owned cars, the alley served as a makeshift playground where children ran, played soccer, and rode bicycles. It was here that Moody spent his last days in China, unaware that his life was about to change forever.

Hong Kong smelled of rain and roasted chestnuts, of sun and dry fish. The streets were crowded, filled with people speaking a Chinese dialect Moody barely recognized, Cantonese, a cousin to the Mandarin he had learned as a child. The city's heartbeat was different from China's mainland. British culture shaped everything, from the stately colonial buildings to the way people dressed. English was the language of business and government, spoken by officials in pressed suits and women in Western-style dresses.

Mami and Moody moved into 225 Wanchai Road, a fourth-floor apartment in a building with no elevator. The Tung family, relatives on Mami's side, had already made a home there. The space was small, but it didn't seem to bother anyone.

At night, the five uncles and Moody rolled out bedding on the floor of the living room, their makeshift sleeping quarters. During the day, the same room became the family's gathering space, then a dining area, then, in the evenings, a place of worship.

Great-grandmother presided over their evening prayers, her voice steady and certain. She had been converted to Christianity by Methodist missionaries in Shandong Province between 1900's eight foreign country's combined military sent the Manchu court fleeting Peking and the Sino-Janpanese war. Her faith never wavered, no matter how many times the family had been forced to flee the advancing Japanese troops.

"Give thanks before every meal," she reminded them.

And so they did.

On Sundays, the entire family would walk or take the trolley to the

Chinese Methodist Church on Hennessy and Johnston Road. Moody rarely missed a service. He listened, but he didn't always understand. He followed the rituals, though he wasn't sure what they meant. Faith was a rhythm, and he moved with it.

Street scene of Queen's Road Central, one block from the Methodist church, where the iconic green colored double decker trolley runs..

Moody's four years in Hong Kong shaped him, though not in ways anyone could see at first. He learned to speak fluent Cantonese for life, adding to his spoken Mandarin skills.

He was quiet, a boy who looked absent-minded in class, always gazing out the window. His younger aunt, Mary, sat beside him in school, her grades always better, her attention never wandering. Teachers assumed

Moody wasn't interested.

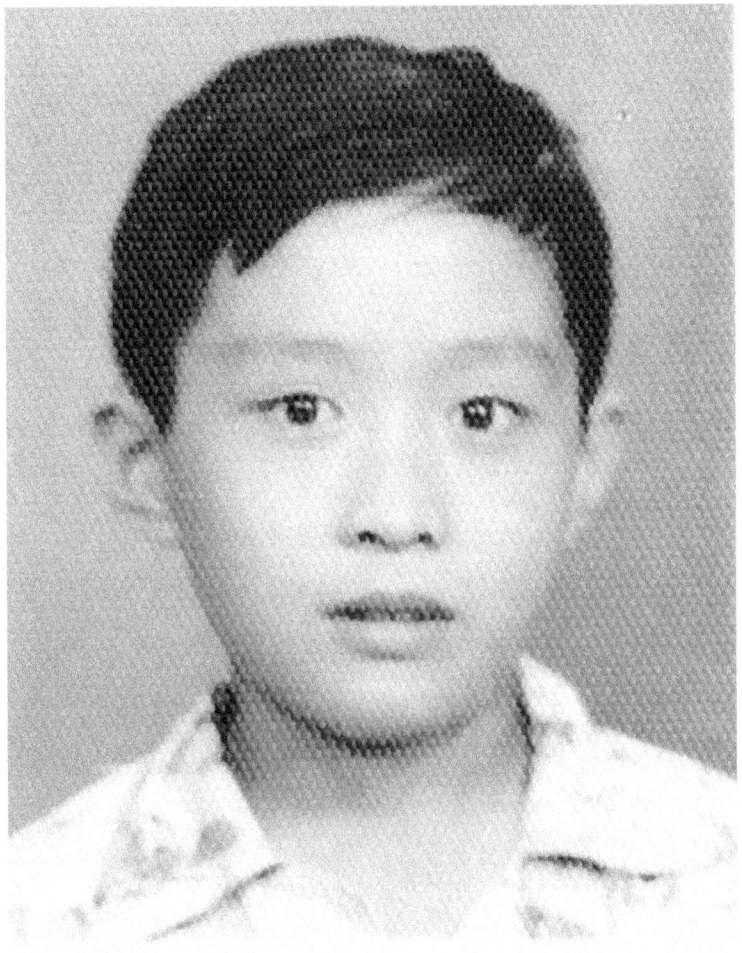

Moody's first known image taken at 7 or 8 years old as a young student learning Chinese in his elementary school years in Hong Kong.

In 1948 Dr. Stephen Tsou travelled to America under a government sponsored medical fellowship. Aileen and Moody were separated from him for the next four years due to People's Republic of China (PRC) having taken control of mainland China and the non-availability of a U.S. Visa. Moody just hoped one day the SS president will take him to

America.

In the imagination of the young boy, maybe someday a big ship like this will take him and Mami to America.

Outside the classroom, he proved them wrong.

One afternoon, a fight broke out in the schoolyard. Moody didn't hesitate; he threw himself into the scuffle, fists swinging. Another altercation erupted during a nature study trip when boys from another school invaded their hillside territory. Stones flew. One struck Moody hard, splitting the skin on the back of his head.

Blood ran down his scalp.

The Uncles were furious. They chased after the boys who had attacked him, but the culprits vanished into the city's endless streets. Mami worried over the wound, pressing a cloth to his head, but Moody didn't flinch. It was just a scratch.

At home, no one scolded him. The elders simply shook their heads and said, "Let him be himself."

There was no pressure for him to change. No rigid expectations. He would grow in his own time. And Mami? She had no regrets about choosing this orphaned boy as her son.

# 5

B y 1949, the world shifted again.

That year, Chairman Mao drove the Nationalist Kuomintang government off the China mainland, forcing them to retreat to Taiwan. China was no longer the country Daddy had left behind. There would be no turning back.

Daddy had already been in America for two years, studying Public Health at Johns Hopkins University. In the upheaval of China's political landscape, he secured a staff physician position at Pennsylvania State Hospital in Coaldale, PA. His work focused on treating coal miners suffering from black lung disease, a slow and suffocating illness.

With his decision to settle in America confirmed, Daddy turned his attention to bringing Mami and Moody across the ocean to unite with him in America.

The U.S. immigration system in the aftermath of World War II was brutally restrictive for would-be Chinese immigrants.

The law allowed only a tiny fraction of applicants to enter, using a complex formula based on outdated census data. Thousands of Chinese families waited years for approval, caught in bureaucratic limbo.

Daddy didn't have years.

He confided in his hospital superintendent, explaining his situation.

By sheer luck, the hospital's district Congressman was the Chairman of the Congressional Immigration Committee. Moved by the family's plight, the Congressman did something extraordinary, he attached Mami and Moody's names as a rider for entry visa to a massive appropriations bill.

The bill passed.

In September 1951, Mami and Moody boarded the SS *President Cleveland* once again. This time sailing toward America.

# 6

They arrived in Coaldale, Pennsylvania, a coal mining town tucked into the mountainous landscape, far removed from the bustling streets of Hong Kong.

It smelled of earth and smoke. The hospital where Daddy worked stood at the town's center, surrounded by small houses coated with coal dust clinging to the windowsills. They moved into a hospital-owned home, where they could draw weekly food rations from the hospital pantry.

The first morning, a visitor arrived, a Presbyterian pastor named Rufus, who had once been a missionary in China. He welcomed the family in broken Mandarin, his smile warm, his presence familiar in a foreign place.

Moody was 11 years and 11 months old. His American life had begun.

The language barrier was immediate. English was nothing like Chinese, it didn't flow the same way, didn't carry the same rhythm. To help him adjust, his parents enrolled him in sixth grade, one year below his Hong Kong grade level, to give him time to learn English.

Moody walks into his Coaldale, PA, sixth grade class room.

Every night, Daddy and Moody read children's books together, Jack and Jill, simple rhymes, and sentences. Moody picked up words quickly, repeating them over and over. At school, his classmates were curious, friendly. A boy named Evan Evans was assigned as his guide.

The school's annual picture day arrived, and Moody stood among his new classmates, caught between two worlds, the boy from China, now an American student.

In 1950, Daddy purchased a black Dodge sedan, his first car in America. It was black, solid, dependable, and a symbol of forward motion. When the snow finally melted that spring, he took the family on weekend road trips, eager to show Moody the country that was now their home. They visited Allentown, Hershey, Philadelphia, New York City, and even Washington, D.C. These short travels helped make this new land feel more familiar.

Daddy had begun to understand that returning to China was no longer a possibility. His new goal was to practice medicine in America outside of government-run facilities. But that dream required a U.S. state medical license. His medical degree from St. John's, a satellite of the University of Pennsylvania, made him eligible to sit for licensure exams after completing a U.S. internship, which was then called the R1 residency.

He applied to the White Plains City General Hospital residency program and was accepted, helped by strong recommendation letters from his professors in Shanghai. Once accepted, the family packed their modest belongings into the Dodge and relocated again, this time to New York City.

# 7

In New York, they found themselves in a common situation for new immigrants with limited means: sharing an apartment. They rented one large room in a shared flat on Morningside Drive on the Upper West Side. The kitchen, living room, and bathrooms were communal, shared with two other families.

Daddy spent his weekdays living at the hospital in the resident quarters. He returned home only on weekends. Mami took a job as a nurse aide at St. Luke's Hospital, a major step down from her wartime role as head nurse in Burma or at Szuchow County Hospital. But she accepted the position without complaint. It was honest work, and the small salary helped increase the household income.

Two months later, with careful budgeting and a few extra dollars earned, the family moved into a small two-bedroom apartment of their own in the same Upper West Side neighborhood.

During that time, Paul was largely unsupervised after school. Fortunately, at age twelve, his basic character and judgment had already been shaped by Great-Grandmother and Mami. He followed a simple set of internal house rules:

- Finish any task you're given, and finish it well
- Return all tools or items where you found them

- Handle incidental small chores as you encounter them
- Don't make excuses. Don't say no to household duties

Paul enrolled at Booker T. Washington Junior High School 54, located on West 107th Street. Like most city schools, it was overcrowded, as families from all over the world had arrived. More than half of Paul's classmates spoke Spanish. The rest spoke a wide range of languages. Paul was placed into eighth grade, his proper level from Hong Kong. His English, while not perfect, matched that of his peers, and he performed better than most in math and science.

New York public schools didn't offer after-school or weekend activities, so Paul kept himself busy. He spent hours at the public library, visited the Museum of Natural History, the Metropolitan Museum, and occasionally saw low-cost matinee movies like *Battle of the North Atlantic*, *Blackboard Jungle*, and *Creature From The Black Lagoon*.

Daddy completed his internship year, the minimum requirement to sit for the state medical board exams. But it was clear the family needed more income, and Daddy needed more time to study for the state medical licensure exam. During this waiting period, positions that paid well without requiring an active state medical license were limited to government jobs.

He found one: the U.S. Public Health Service was hiring physicians for the Indian Health Hospital in Albuquerque, New Mexico. The job fit his background and qualifications. He applied and was accepted.

None of them had ever been to the Southwest. Paul looked at a map. New Mexico felt like a faraway land. In the 1950s, Albuquerque had a population of just over half a million. Known for its role in World War II atomic weapons development, it had grown quickly. Two-thirds of the city's residents had migrated from the East Coast to work in federal jobs or to support local communities.

By the middle of the summer, the family boarded a plane and headed west. They rented a modest house close to Daddy's hospital and Paul's new middle school, the Jefferson Junior High School.

Albuquerque brought space, dry air, and quiet. Paul, still an only child, had moved so frequently that long-term friendships hadn't had time to form. He had no regular playmates and no close social circle. He read. He studied. He spent time alone.

He tried track and basketball at Jefferson Junior High, but quickly discovered he was too short, too slow, and too clumsy. His athletic performance peaked as a second-string player on the JJHS school basketball team. But he didn't feel sorry for himself.

Jefferson Junior High School basketball team photo. Paul realized he is too short, too slow, and very clumsy to play basketball or any school competition sport.

In class, Paul did well, often better than the children of professionals. He moved on to Highland High School, where he kept to his studies. He was the only Chinese student there. Most of his classmates spoke perfect English; many others were Hispanic.

The school was surrounded by vacant lots. On windy days, tumbleweeds rolled across the empty spaces. Paul walked or biked to school every day. Buses weren't provided.

Outside of school, Paul found work. He washed dishes at Lobo Joe's, a popular restaurant. Occasionally, he worked at a Chinese restaurant as a short-order cook. After saving enough, he bought a used Sears-brand Vespa-style scooter. It spent more time in the repair shop than on the road.

The experience taught him:

- Never buy cheap scooters.
- Learn to drive a manual transmission car.
- When you can, buy only new toys, select ones that have lowest failure rate.

Later, the Highland basketball coach made Paul the junior team manager. He traveled with the team to in-state games and, occasionally, across the border to El Paso, Texas.

Academically, Paul stayed on course. He took summer classes and AP-level coursework in math and science. These extra units would help him enroll one grade level higher when the family eventually moved to California.

Still, Paul kept a low profile. He attended social functions but stayed on the edges of activities. He didn't improve his dancing skills, and his English, though improving, still bore an accent. He never tried to show off.

This image is Paul's Highland High 1957 year book front cover. He departed from Highland of Albuquerque, NM, in summer of 1957. He never returned for his 1958 original class year book photo session.

While Paul focused on school, Daddy was preparing for the next step. Each evening, he studied preparatory books on how to pass the California state medical board licensure exam. He was determined, focused, and ready. When the time came, he sat for the exam, and passed on the first attempt.

With his California license in hand, he applied for the position of Superintendent at the Hassler Health home, part of the City and County of San Fransico Health System, located in Redwood City, about 30 miles south of San Francisco. The facility had long been run by an aging physician who could no longer manage its day-to-day operations. The position required a steady hand, medical knowledge and experience. Daddy was appointed and gladly accepted.

In late 1955, Great-Grandmother traveled from Hong Kong to join the family in Albuquerque. A few months later, in the summer of 1956, the family packed up once again, this time bound for California. It felt different. More permanent. They believed this would be home. That feeling held true for decades to come.

The Hassler Health Home was perched on a hill off Edgewood Road, accessible only by a narrow, winding two-lane, hilly road. The hospital operated an eight passenger station wagon that made regular shuttle trips into town during the workday. Paul used the shuttle for school, library and city errands.

He enrolled as a 12th-grade student at Sequoia High School. The school didn't question the extra year gained from his coursework gained in New Mexico. His records from Highland High were accepted without issue, and Sequoia registered him as a senior. He graduated that same year.

# 8

Paul was now a high school graduate, but still uncertain about his future college education. He and his parents knew very little about the structure of higher education in the United States. There were no college counselors, no family friends to guide him. He didn't know which colleges were considered good, which majors were in demand, or how the college application process worked.

By default, and with no fanfare, he applied to San Jose State College. He hand-carried his application and documents. They accepted him for the fall semester of 1958. He enrolled as a full-time day student. The daily commute was 23.3 miles each way, by the Southern Pacific commuter train in the morning and train to return home in the evening. The trains were crowded with students like him, eager, quiet, tired, and focused.

Paul had begun to connect the dots of his life. He remembered how hard his parents had worked in New York to build a future for him. He knew he wasn't physically strong enough to be a laborer. He had no taste for shortcuts. He wanted to earn his place. He knew he did well in school. He had escaped alone from a children's dormitory at age four. He had reacted with force to a needle injection as a toddler. These were signs of independence. Resilience.

He would not disappoint his parents.

Still, Paul didn't yet have a clear vision of his profession. Medicine hadn't yet emerged as his only path. But it was all around him. Both of his parents were in the medical field. By default, and without knowing much about other options, he began preparing for medical school.

He took a full load of science and math courses. He enjoyed the structure, the clarity of those subjects. He also found joy in the liberal arts, art history, and music, especially. These were his pleasures.

After his first year at San Jose State, he started to hear more from classmates about Stanford University. They said it was better. Stronger. He applied in the middle of his second year, and he was accepted. The commute on the same train was shortened to 4.8 miles one way. He took the train to Palo Alto, then biked the last half mile to campus.

At Stanford, the coursework was heavier. Organic chemistry. Embryology. Psychology. Paul had little time for socializing, and his English courses continued to be placed in the "non-native speaker" category. All three of his college years had followed that pattern.

Paul wasn't passionate about medicine yet. He didn't feel a calling, not the kind people spoke about in interviews or personal statements. But he learned that some medical schools accepted students after only three years of undergraduate study, if they had enough credits and met admission requirements.

Paul applied to four schools: University of California San Francisco, Stanford, UCLA, and Baylor. UCLA and Baylor rejected him immediately because he hadn't yet earned or scheduled to earn a bachelor's degree. But UCSF and Standford both offered him conditional admission.

Stanford's offer came with a strict condition: He would need to enroll as an MD/PhD combined program candidate. UCSF asked only for a quick in-person interview, which was conducted by the chairman of neurosurgery in between the interviewer's surgeries, half in scrubs, half in a lab coat.

Paul chose UCSF.

UNIVERSITY OF CALIFORNIA
SAN FRANCISCO MEDICAL CENTER

FALL SEMESTER 1961

REGISTRATION CARD

School, College, Division, Course

TSOU                    PAUL    MOODY

Family name        First given name        Middle name

Fees paid

Student's
Signature

Paul's UCSF student ID card from his first semester of medical school registration which cost about $125. This was good for admission to system wide activities. No other mandatory fees required, including no tuition.

Aileen and Stephen Tsou, Paul's proud parents, in front of their Hassler Health home superintendent's residence in Redwood city, CA.

Paul's 1965 Medical school class students gathered in the Toland Hall amphitheater lecture hall for a class didactic lecture.

Paul promised his parents he would dress up for his doctorate graduation ceremony and take photos with parents and friends.

# 9

Paul told his parents about his choice of profession and the school he would attend. They were happily surprised. More importantly, it confirmed something they had quietly hoped for: Paul had reached a meaningful milestone. He wasn't aimless after all. The acceptance came about ten months before the start of medical school. With the pressure off, Paul loosened up a little. That summer, he still worked six weeks as a temporary landscape gardener for the Sunnyvale Union School District.

In the 1960s, tuition for the University of California professional schools was low or nil. In fact, at the beginning of that decade, there was no official "tuition" at all, only a small incidental fee of about $120 -150 per semester, as a student activity fee. A student ID gave you free access to all UC interscholastic games, football, basketball, and more.

There was no need to buy a microscope. The school loaned each student one for the entire freshman year. This was the era before digital images, genome sequencing, or multimedia instruction. Everything was hands-on.

UCSF was now the only medical school located within the city of San Francisco. By the time Paul began, the school had moved all of its basic science classes from Berkeley to the new Medical Sciences Building on the Parnassus campus. Its former city rival, Stanford, had already relocated its entire medical school operation to Palo Alto, in the southern part of the San Francisco Peninsula.

The 1960s marked the dawn of the high-tech industry, and the San Francisco Peninsula was becoming its epicenter. The University of California, San Francisco School of Medicine still relied on traditional teaching methods at the time, its curriculum had not yet embraced the emerging high-tech approaches seen in other disciplines. The main campus sat on the slope of Mount Parnassus, with several key structures housing the basic science departments and clinical hospital buildings. The north-facing façade of the complex overlooked Golden Gate Park.

Just across the street, built on a lower level, was the Millberry Union, home to student union, dormitories, dining areas, meeting rooms, a basketball court, swimming pool, and the campus bookstore. Most importantly, the lower-level elevator provided quick access to the N-Judah streetcar line, which connected the Parnassus campus directly to downtown Market Street and ended at the Embarcadero. Paul had entered a new world.

Two other freshmen in Paul's class who also studied at San Jose State College: Dan McDaniel and Norman Pugh. The rest of the incoming students were mostly from the San Francisco Bay Area and the City of Los Angeles. Among them were three honorably discharged military pilots, two graduates of East Coast Ivy League schools, and one Christian missionary who wanted to add medical skills to care for her converts in Africa.

Paul shared a dorm room with his friend Dan McDaniel, whom he had known from their San Jose State days when they rode the morning train together to campus. Dan had also completed three years at San

Jose State before being accepted. Once the semester began, there wasn't much time to talk. Both Paul and Dan studied alone and didn't participate in the group study sessions.

Classes ran from 8 AM to 5 PM, with a one-hour break for lunch. Gross anatomy took up much of the time, dissecting cadavers in the lab. Some classmates stayed late into the night. Some worked part-time in the labs. Others couldn't bear it at all. Three students left the program altogether within the first two weeks of classes, unable to handle the sights or the smell of formaldehyde.

During the first anatomy course, their histology professor, Dr. Simpson, passed away from cancer. Before her death, she had willed her body to the university. When her cadaveric body appeared on the dissection table, the entire class stood in silence. They paid their respects, deeply moved, an image Paul would carry within him for a long time.

For the histology course, each student was issued a microscope and several boxes of histologic specimens mounted on glass slides. Paul and the rest of the students did their histology homework in the peace and quiet of their dorm rooms. The chemistry course was only moderately difficult for Paul. It was taught by a well-published professor, Dr. Ganon, MD, PhD.

Biochemistry was harder for Paul to grasp. His initial poor grade reflected his struggle with the subject. A panel of his basic science professors met with him to discuss the situation and to try to understand the root cause. The issue was resolved after Paul spent more time working with the professor's teaching assistant. From then on, he did well in biochemistry.

In the second year, classroom learning was blended with early exposure to clinical medicine. The students learned to perform physical examinations on real patients at Laguna Honda Hospital, a long-term care facility. Later, they were introduced to the San Francisco General Hospital, where they would eventually train in emergency medicine. These hospitals were about five miles apart but separated by hilly terrain and ran through very different neighborhoods.

Paul mentioned to his parents that he would need a reliable way to travel between hospitals. They bought him a 1962 Volkswagen Beetle. It served many purposes: getting to training rotations, visiting home, maybe even giving Paul a small boost in social standing. His parents were concerned that he still hadn't developed strong social instincts. They hoped the car might help.

The second half of the second year was more hands-on. At San Francisco General Hospital, students followed house staff on rounds, learning how to observe and interact with patients. At Laguna Honda, they practiced bedside examination skills under supervision.

The school's physical diagnosis class had a long history. The instructor was Dr. John Moe, then in his 80s, who had chaired the course for over four decades. This was not yet the era of computer courses or artificial intelligence. Dr. Moe emphasized diagnosing illness through careful history, physical exam, and a few basic lab tests. Dr. Moe's percentage of diagnosable diseases accuracy was surprisingly high, even without the aid of checking a computer for extensive blood test results, image findings, and AI analysis, or group study consensus. Every student received a copy of Dr. Moe's hand-written pertinent method and findings on the diseases and their agnostic impressions.

By the third year, Paul and his classmates rotated through all major clinical services. They learned in the emergency medicine department, the acute psychiatric ward, and the surgical floors. For the first time, they were allowed to examine and care for patients, always under supervision. Students were teamed with residents, including during night shifts. A good student was the one who jumped out of bed first when a case came in and reported back their findings to the supervising resident.

In the summers between two school years, six to eight student research fellowships were available to those who applied. Paul applied and was accepted for all three summer student research fellowships. The first summer, he worked in Dr. John Mone's anatomy lab, studying the effects of chemicals on fetal development in rats. The embryos were sliced into thin sections, mounted on slides, studied for abnormalities, and catalogued. In the second summer fellowship, he studied renal function under Dr. Carolyn Peel.

The third summer was the most fun for Paul. During this time, he investigated parasite infestation in an under-12-year-old pediatric age group. The children were of the Chinese Hakai ethnic group, boat dwellers living on their wooden sampans at the Hong Kong Yau Ma De Typhoon Shelter. The research was conducted aboard a non-profit clinic boat moored at the Yau Ma Dee Typhoon Shelter. During this time, Paul stayed with a family friend across the harbor and enjoyed weekend social events. At summer's end, he submitted his epidemiology findings.

In the fourth year of medical school, almost all students began to firm up which electives they would take. Class members were also starting to think about and plan for their next steps after graduation. There was finally time for small talk among classmates. Within the formal structure of medical education, fourth-year students were free to choose from a wide range of electives. The effort required for each elective varied between very little and deep intellectual engagement. Paul's two chosen electives were cardiology and pulmonary function studies.

The application season for internships came in the fourth year. Paul applied for rotating internships that combined medicine and surgery. His top choices were San Francisco General Hospital, Harbor Hospital in Los Angeles, and UCSF's own Moffitt Hospital. He matched his first choice, San Francisco General.

In preparation for the long hours of internship, Paul rented a room in an elderly woman's home near the hospital. Close enough to walk. Before graduation, Paul promised his parents he would participate in the graduation ceremony and wear the full cap and gown. It would be the first time they saw him graduate. They attended, along with a few relatives, in May of 1965. He never told them he had quietly skipped high school and college (UCSF awards BS college degree to the three-year admittees after completion of the first year of Medical school) ceremonies. This time, he stood on stage, diploma in hand.

# Part Two:

Overview

# 10

From 1965 to 1966, important milestones came and went. In the summer of 1965, a life-changing event emerged for Paul: He passed the California State Medical Board licensure exam. The certificate would be sent to him at the end of his internship (R1) year. Around the same time, the Selective Service issued command orders to all eligible males, especially those in the medical profession. For medical professionals, there were two pathways to serve the country. One was immediate activation into uniformed service after internship.

The second was delayed activation, allowed only after completing an approved specialty residency. Those who chose the delay were allowed to select which branch of service they preferred. Paul selected delayed activation through the U.S. Public Health Service program and chose pathology as his specialty. He signed the Selective Service documents, committing to this pathway. At the time, Paul knew little about pathology, but he believed it might offer a deeper understanding of disease processes. He had also spoken with two classmates who had already committed to pathology as their future specialty.

Paul worked long hours as an intern, R1, at San Francisco General Hospital, but he still found time on his off weekends to go skiing at Squaw Valley's Sugar Bowl near Lake Tahoe. A life-changing event happened on one of those snowy slopes. His skiing skill was no match for the unforgiving icy terrain. He took a fall while skiing downhill, his skis crossed, and he twisted his right knee. Paul managed to get up and hobble down the slope. He then drove himself back to the Emergency Room at SFGH. His friends in the ER called the Chief of Orthopaedics, Dr. Ted Boville, to evaluate him. The diagnosis: a severe medial collateral ligament sprain of the right knee. The treatment at the time, reflective of that bygone era, was hospitalization and suspension in traction for the injured leg.

Dr. Boville was kind and unhurried. He answered Paul's questions, not only about the condition of his knee, but also about his profession in orthopaedics. Paul was back at work three days after the incident. Soon after, he wrote a letter to the United States Public Health and Human Resources (USPHS) Department to cancel his commitment to the delayed service pathway. He no longer wanted to pursue pathology. Instead, he opted for immediate activation after internship and would try applying for an orthopaedic residency program, to start after his Selective Services obligation has completed. The USPHS granted his change request. Paul's parents were horrified at this change but kept their opinions to themselves.

Image of USPHS Logo

Paul was now the property of the U.S. Public Health Service, starting on July 1, 1966. Paul like most of the young USPHS general medical officers, assume they will be comfortably posted in a hospital or a clinic environment for the next two years. Paul likewise, was ill-informed. the USPHS doctor is regularly send its commissioned medical providers to the natural disaster areas, of domestic or foreign origin, shipped out on large US Coast Guard cutters, Indian reservations, or to any one of the military services during war.. Paul's first assignment was the USPHS Outpatient Clinic in Houston, Texas, a good post.. There wasn't much time to prepare for the sudden shift in location, culture, work rules, and uniform etiquette. The printed rule of two weeks of uniform training was waived. Fortunately, the most up-to-date medical information was available equally to civilian practitioners and those in uniform. Paul was hastily fitted for his service uniform, unsure of what the next assignment might bring. The biggest change, yet to come? The pace of medicine was slow. And everyone called him "Sir." How strange! Still, Paul adapted quickly to the new role.

Paul settled into the Houston USPHS clinic, located in the downtown district. The staff was small, just two other medical personnel. The higher -ranking doctor, a general surgeon near retirement, barely spoke beyond a few necessary polite words. The other staff member was a mid-career, unmarried pharmacist still looking for fun and adventure around town and everywhere else. He and Paul once drove to New Orleans for a long weekend to enjoy the live jazz music at the reservation Hall.

Good times, Paul would learn, don't always last long for a junior uniformed doctor.

The next assignment came, unsurprisingly, just three months after

Paul arrival in Houston, Texas. New orders were issued. They read: "You are to report to the *U.S. Coast Guard Cutter Spencer* (WPG-36), Staten Island, NY. Report date no later than seven days from the date of this order."

Paul made it aboard the *USCGC Spencer* just in time, shortly before the Cutter set sail out of New York Harbor, bound for her assigned ocean station in the middle of the Atlantic Ocean. At just 23 years old, Paul held the rank of full lieutenant. Onboard, only the Captain and the Chief Engineer outranked him.

Lieutenant Paul Tsou aboard the *USCG Cutter Spencer*, a much decorated World War Two, convoy vessel. Credited for one solo effort and two combined action in the demise of enemy submarines.

Paul was a newcomer to the United States Coast Guard, let alone to a battle-hardened Cutter. The *Spencer* was painted grey, a visual reminder of her transfer to the Navy during World War II. The *USCGC Spencer* was a well-decorated warship; she sank one enemy submarine on her own and was credited with assisting in the sinking of at least two others. Imagine the number of Allied sailors she saved, and the countless supply ships she kept out of harm's way.

*Spencer's* assignment was one month of mid-Atlantic Ocean Station duty, an old World War II legacy, originally created to provide a protective submarine screen and pick up survivors from torpedoed Allied vessels. One week of the month was spent sailing to Hamilton, Bermuda, docking at the British Navy shipyard for resupply and rest. After completing his first Coast Guard tour, Paul returned to the Houston USPHS medical clinic. He didn't have to wait long before the next set of Coast Guard orders arrived.

# 12

T he new order instructed Paul to report to the USCG *Bering Strait* (WPEC-382) no later than December 1, 1966, at the Honolulu Sand Island U.S. Coast Guard Pacific District base. "Complete and update your personal affairs before the start of this tour," the order further read. It sounded like an unusually long tour.

The ink schematic profile image of the *USCG cutter Bering Strait*. Offered in the 1966 vessel's Christmas card. An unknown crew member contributed to this art.

Paul packed what little he owned and drove his Volkswagen back to San Francisco. He had a few free days to spend with his parents. They were worried, though they didn't show their anxiety. During this short window, Paul managed to send out his orthopaedic residency applications to UCSF, UCLA, and Stanford. He asked Dr. Ted Boville to be one of his references.

Paul reported to the Sand Island base in Honolulu on time. The Cutter still needed more time in port for preparations before departure. The *USCG Cutter Bering Strait* (WHEC-382) was formerly a U.S. Navy World War II tender for small seaplanes. An inquiry into the vessel's duty history revealed that she was originally designed and built in the late 1930s as a tender for small seaplanes. But near the end of WWII, she took on a new role as lead search-and-rescue ship for the U.S. Army Air Forces' returning B-29 Superfortress bombers. After completing their bombing runs over Japan, many of these aircraft sustained various degrees of damage, some planes had to ditch near Saipan due to running out of fuel, mechanical failure, or combat damage. The *Bering Strait* rescued full crews, twelve airmen per plane, from at least two B-29s, and many partial crews from others that didn't make it back for various reasons.

The *Bering Strait* was transferred to the Coast Guard within the two years prior to Paul's assignment. Her alphanumeric designation changed with the transfer and again when her duty function was updated. After her transfer to the U.S. Coast Guard, the *Bering Strait* underwent several modifications. Hoses were rerouted to better serve smaller vessels. Quarters were refurbished to accommodate guests. The aft-mounted second five-inch gun was removed. For her new, though not yet officially disclosed, tropical destination, air conditioning units were installed. Throughout the ship, .50 caliber machine guns were mounted around the deck.

Eventually, the Cutters' specific duty assignment was announced. The *Bering Strait* would serve in South Vietnam, the exact location not yet specified, as a tender for close-support vessels, commonly known as "Swift Boats". The official operational name was Patrol Craft Fast (PCF). These Swift Boats were about 50 feet long, powered by twin diesel engines that could push their top speed to 37 miles per hour. Each boat was armed with two .50 caliber machine guns, one of which was co-mounted with an 81mm mortar, and staffed by a crew of five Navy sailors.

After completing a 24-hour patrol in the delta rivers, the Swift Boats would return to the Cutter for crew change and replenishment. The returning crew rested aboard while fresh teams departed, deployed. From 1966 to 1968, the Coast Guard Cutters and Navy destroyer escorts rotated through duty along the southern coastline of Vietnam. At the end of that period, a new group of Cutters was reassigned to Cam Ranh Bay, farther to the north.

For this group of Cutters, according to the official Navy logs, the USCG Cutter *Spencer* held station at Cam Ranh Bay for nine months in 1969. One notable entry recorded that Lieutenant John Kerry, who would later became U.S. Secretary of State, received medical treatment aboard the *Spencer* for a leg wound. For his actions during the war, Kerry was awarded three Purple Hearts, one Navy Silver Star, and one Bronze Star for valor.

The Swift Boats received no greater publicity than in the 1979 movie "*Apocalypse Now*". The film, which was over three hours in length, followed a swift boat crew that lived and died on their boat. Their mission was to locate and kill the rogue Lt. Colonel Kurtz. The river they traveled was filled with danger: Viet Cong projectiles, tigers, tribal spears, and other lethal weapons.

During the 1966 to 1967 period the southern most coastal zone the US vessels were tasked to provide gun fire support of the land based unites and provide daily tender replenishment of the 24 hours rotating swift boat crew and on board food and munition. The swift boats patrol the river in pairs.

A team of two Swift Boats moored together along side of *Bering Strait* in their 24 hours stop over. Crew in final preparation for departure, hoisted the Stars and Stripes proudly. An in coming Swift is waiting in the background.

Back view of two Swift Boats moored together along side of *Bering Strait* in their 24 hour stop over.

Paul's daily duties aboard the Cutter were mostly routine. Each morning began with sick call. The NCO medical chief handled the majority of these cases, except after an R&R or dry dock port calls. Following stops in Olongapo (Philippines), Hong Kong, and Sasebo (Japan), sick call lines grew noticeably longer. Some of these ports carried a reputation, others had physical evidence of their notoriety.

There were a few minor injuries and occasional concerns about possible infectious diseases. Even the ship's executive officer came to see Paul once the morning rush of sick call had quieted down. Throughout his time aboard, Paul treated just one Vietnamese fisherman with a medical condition and another who had sustained a wrist fracture, his first opportunity to apply a long arm cast.

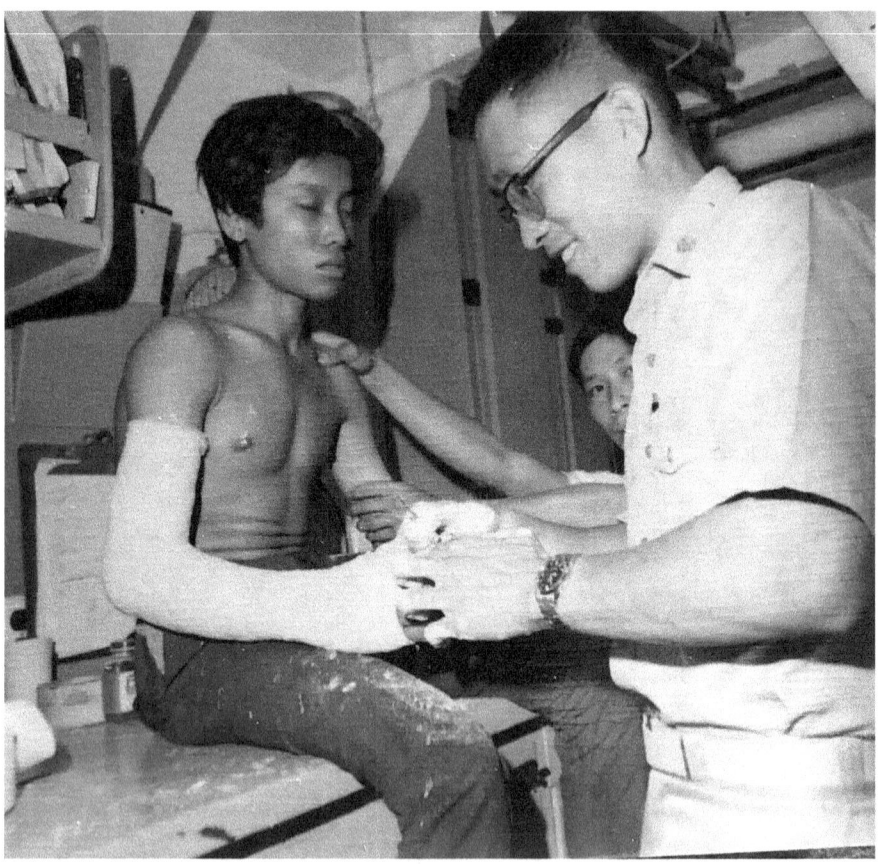

The *Bering Strait*, while on patrol, answered a medical call to assist a young Vietnamese fisherman who fell from a ladder a few miles from shore. The fisherman was taken aboard and his injured wrist x-rayed. Lieutenant Tsou made the diagnosis of a distal radius fracture. He put on a long arm cast after closed reduction. The injuried was quickly returned to his fishing boat.

One of the most joyful moments came when he met a group of young Vietnamese children on Dai Phu Quoc Island. South Vietnamese and

Thai fishing vessels also operated in the same waters, and from time to time, sick or injured fishermen were allowed aboard the Cutter for treatment. One fisherman presented with an acute cardiac condition, which Paul managed with antihypertensives and diuretics before returning him back to his boat. Paul performed his first orthopaedic procedure, a long arm plaster cast for a wrist fracture, on a young Vietnamese fisherman in the sick bay of the *USCG Cutter Bering Strait.*

The author was entertained by the children of Dai Phu Duai Island, Vietnam. No hostilities on the Vietemese southern most land mass.

Beginning of the end. Paul on deck of the *Bering Strait* on her last day of last patrol. The relief Cutter in the back ground.

The Coast Guard Cutters assigned to South Vietnam were tasked with patrolling specific patches of water and carrying out designated duties for a duration of four to six weeks per vessel, until officially relieved. During its nine-month deployment, the *Bering Strait* underwent one dry dock period for below-the-waterline repairs at the Subic Bay Naval Yard in the Philippines.

Additional time was spent in the Eastern Pacific for R&R, port calls in Singapore, Kaohsiung, and Sasebo, each lasting about a week. A special highlight of the tour was the *Bering Strait's* assignment as the Hong Kong Station Ship for one month. In this role, the Cutter's duty was to receive and transmit all official U.S. military messages for American vessels in the Hong Kong area.

Paul in dress whites on deck of *Bering Strait* in Hong Kong harbor. The Cutter was posted as a US station ship for one month.

During the visit to Hong Kong, Paul was re-acquainted with his four uncles who still lived in the British Colony. The crew was especially happy about this assignment, several members were able to have their spouse fly out to Hong Kong to reunite and spend a few days together. After completing the Hong Kong station duty, the *Bering Strait* was assigned two additional war zone tours in Vietnamese waters.

At the end of the final two tours, the crew was happy, looking forward to see their loved ones soon on U.S. soil. The *Bering Strait* made one final stop at the Subic Bay Naval facility for fuel and provisions before beginning the trans-Pacific journey home. Paul was even happier. He asked for, and was granted, permission not to make the return voyage with the Cutter. Instead, he would use the ten-day transit window to visit his maternal grand mother in Taipei, Taiwan, and then fly back to

Honolulu just before the *Bering Strait* sails into Sand Island Coast Guard Base. The captain reluctantly granted Paul's request. Every detail of Paul's individualized travel plan worked out without mishaps. While the Cutter was at sea, Paul spent one week visiting his grandmother in Taipei. There were only two weeks left in his Selective Service obligation. Paul chose to spend his remaining time working at the USPHS outpatient clinic at the San Francisco Hospital.

# Part Three:

Residency, Fellowship & the New Beginnings

# 13

Orthopaedic surgery residency at UCSF began for Paul on July 1, 1968. He attended the department chairman, Dr. Don Lucas's welcome party just days before, meeting his fellow incoming residents. Among them, Paul was the only graduate from the University of California; the others came from Tennessee, Iowa, Minnesota, Ohio, and Washington State. Each new resident received this four-year rotation schedule. Paul noticed that his time at the San Francisco main campus was limited to a single six-month rotation limited to total joint replacement. He raised no objection. Perhaps the department believed the out-of-state in coming residents needed more exposure to San Francisco's medical and cultural environment, while Paul, already familiar with the city, did not.

All residents gathered one afternoon per week at the main campus for didactic classroom teaching. This mandatory half-day session was dedicated to the fundamentals of orthopaedic musculoskeletal disease and trauma. Emphasis was also placed on basic biomechanics and tumors. The purpose of these sessions was to establish a shared baseline of knowledge among all residents. Any further learning beyond that would depend on the individual's own effort and imagination.

Back in uniform again. This time in the UCSF resident's white coat. Standing on the front steps of the Parnassus Campus Medical Science Building, where all the orthopaedic residents gathered every Tuesday afternoon for required instruction.

Looking back, Paul believes that on each of his rotations, he had outstanding mentors, both senior residents and professors, who shaped his path and taught him the traditional principles of orthopaedics. One rotation, in particular, gave him more than just knowledge. It gave him the chance to meet his future wife, Schumarry Chao. Any other rotation would not have created the same setting for their meeting and their romance to unfold. That fateful meeting, Paul believes, could only have been arranged by God. The resulting marriage has lasted fifty-four years, and counting.

His first year of residency combined research and pediatric orthopaedic care at the Sonoma State Hospital. This facility served children with severe physical and intellectual disabilities. It was located 40 miles north of the Golden Gate Bridge. Since Paul was unmarried at the time, he chose to live in the hospital staff quarters. He only left the hospital grounds for didactic sessions and the occasional weekend.

His attending physician, Dr. Robert Samuelson, proved to be an excellent mentor in clinical research. Though not a standout in surgical skill, Dr. Samuelson taught Paul how to design scientific research project, after collected the data write the paper, and submit the findings for publication. Paul wrote his first research paper under Dr. Samuelson's guidance. That paper on hip dislocation in cerebral palsy of children, published in 1972. Dr. Samuelson also taugh paul how to dictate clairly in the process improve his spoken English.

Chief resident John Sellman also left an impression. John never avoided work. He quietly picked up unfinished tasks and took on extra duties without complaint. His advice to junior residents included the following: never avoid work, choose cases that offer the best clinical experience, always complete what you start, and never show off in front of a group.

# 14

The first six months of Paul's second-year rotation took place at Merritt Hospital in the East Bay. This was his first real exposure to orthopaedic private clinic practice. All the orthopaedic surgeons on staff took part in teaching a single junior resident. Paul followed each practitioner on hospital rounds, responded on the first calls for the Emergency Room on the attending's behalf, and served as first assistant in surgery. These were mostly bread-and-butter orthopaedic cases.

One surgeon's teaching left an unforgettable impression on Paul. Dr. Jack Tupper was a hand surgeon who specialized in microsurgical techniques for severed limb replantation. He showed Paul how to re-anastomose tiny veins, arteries, and nerves; some severed vassels were less than one millimeter in diameter. Using a microscope, Dr. Tupper demonstrated how to handle the fine/small tools and almost invisible and drifting sutures required for these delicate procedures.

A few parting social words before moving on to the next rotation. At a Christmas party near Moffitt Hospital, a cardiology fellow originally from Honolulu asked Paul to look up his family while he was in Hawaii. "They'll show you around Honolulu," he promised. At another year-end family gathering, a friend reminded Paul that her family was planning a vacation to Hawaii in the coming year, and made sure he knew he'd be expected to play tour guide for all the islands tours.

Paul's next two six-month rotations took place in Honolulu, Hawaii. He flew there carrying just a single duffle bag, and came back with a lifelong sweetheart. A firm commitment of heart and legal marriage followed in less than ten months after his arrival in Honolulu.

For that entire year, 12 months, Paul's rotation site was in Hawaii. The department typically reserved these six-month assignments, or two consecutive rotations, for single, unmarried residents. Married residents could still apply, but selection was never guaranteed. Even if requested, there was only a 50/50 chance of being assigned the Honolulu rotation.

Paul arrived at Tripler Army Hospital, the first of the two rotations, the day before the start of his island residency. His assigned housing was in the hospital's bachelor quarters, simple apartment units. The outgoing UCSF resident, Jack Parker, passed down his barely running, rusty Ford Falcon convertible to Paul. The next day, Paul reported to the Chairman of Orthopaedics, a Colonel, and the executive Lt. Colonel and began his work routine.

The entire professional staff was welcoming and supportive. It was immediately clear, to Paul and to everyone else, that Tripler's own residents were very knowledgeable and far more experienced in surgical technique compared to Paul. However, the UCSF residents had a slight edge in book knowledge.

While there, Paul was granted all the privileges of all military bases: access to PXs, restaurants, and recreational facilities across the island. Several wounded Vietnam War veterans from Hawaii were under the care of the orthopaedic service, including one who would later become the U.S. Secretary of Veterans Affairs.

# 15

During his third year, the first six months of residency at Queen's Hospital, Honolulu's premier private medical center, more fateful events unfolded. It was here that Paul gained hands-on experience with the emerging technique of anterior cervical spine surgery, learning directly from Dr. Ralph Coward and Dr. Gabriel Ma. And it was here, on the grounds of Queen's Hospital and later on the beaches of Waikiki, that he met his future wife, Schumarry Chao.

Queen's Hospital, founded by the last reigning monarch of Hawaii, is nestled on the lower slopes near the Pali Highway and Punchbowl Crater. Paul moved into a nearby apartment just off the sloping hillside, sharing it with two other residents from Tripler Army Hospital.

At Queen's, the orthopaedic and neurosurgical private practitioners had taken on the responsibility of teaching the rotating residents. Their instruction included bedside rounds, surgical assisting, and answering emergency calls alongside the mentors. Fortunately, Paul's previous six months at Tripler had given him enough orthopaedic experience to manage the general trauma cases admitted to Queen's with confidence.

By this point in his training, Paul was now the senior resident on rotation, supervising one junior resident, Dr. Tom Grollman.

The new surgical technique of anterior cervical spine surgery was a newly introduced technique in the worldwide spine community at the time. Paul acquired his early experience in this procedure while serving as first assistant to two renowned surgeons: Dr. Ralph Coward and Dr. Gabriel Ma. Each had developed their own proprietary spinal instrumentation and implants.

Dr. Coward was highly protective of the operative field. He did not allow residents to handle retractors or insert any instruments below the surface of the wound, aiming to avoid any potential intra-operative mishaps caused by the inexperience of his residents. Dr. Ma, on the other hand, was more permissive; he allowed residents greater hands-on involvement with the surgical instruments during the procedure.

At Queens, he met Schumarry. Their first encounter was in an elevator, no words, just a casual glance. Later that morning, they met again in the radiology reading room. Dr. Glauber Liese, the department chair, joked that surely they'd met before in San Francisco. They hadn't. But that moment was the start. By lunchtime, they crossed paths again, strangers no more. They shared a table, then many more. Walks on the beach. Long talks. Paul had no idea that Schumarry had already cleared her social calendar for him, canceling previous dates, including one with his own junior resident, Doctor Thomas Grollman.

Paul's pace of learning orthopaedics and spine surgery was fast and detailed. Even faster, though, was how quickly the young Paul and Schumarry began learning about each other's lives. Paul recalled the furious pace. Their next encounter came soon enough, at lunch the very same day, over a free meal at Queen's Hospital cafeteria. As soon as they saw each other in the crowded room full of hungry young professionals, they made their way straight toward one another. Before heading off to their next scheduled tasks, they made arrangements for a more private conversation moment.

Schumarry and Paul continued get to know each other more on the Waikiki beach. A beautiful place to spend time together.

Those conversations continued on the beach and at local hangouts. During his time in Hawaii, Paul knew very little about Schumarry's prior social calendar, but it became clear that it had once been very full. Yet, whenever Paul called her up for lunch or invited her to see a martial arts movie, she seemed to be free and unhurried. This was due to her already cleared social commitments. Among the cancelled plans was a previously arranged outing to the Polynesian Cultural Center with Paul's junior orthopaedic resident, Thomas Grollman, son of a well-published radiology text book. Her excuse to others for backing out was simple, though admittedly a little embarrassing. Dr. Grollman didn't speak to either of them for years afterward.

Paul's social history was close to nonexistent. So why the buzz around this Chinese female medical student? Schumarry eventually admitted, in her typically understated way, that she had recently been crowned Miss Chinatown Los Angeles. News like that traveled fast, on both sides of the Pacific. Paul, who rarely read the local newspaper, had no idea. The title had introduced Schumarry to Asian and other communities across the coasts.

But for Paul, it wasn't about her title. He was drawn to her in deeper, more essential ways. Her personality was worlds apart from his. People liked being around her. She was intelligent, sharp, direct, and rarely hid her feelings. She was generous with friends, and, of course, blessed with natural beauty. Paul believed that what attracted Schumarry to him was, perhaps, his simplicity. Unlike the polished or privileged suitors her family may have imagined for her, Paul came plainly wrapped. Tear off the wrapping, and here was a 28-year-old man, with only three years of college, two years of service in the Coast Guard, and who knew his way around the Pacific, had no inherited wealth, but could give clear direction in a few concise words. His intelligence, cloaked in humility, seemed to be his greatest asset. Schumarry understood that she was going against her parents' wishes to spend time with someone who, on the surface, had little to offer by traditional standards. But what she saw in Paul was enough.

There were other attributes in Paul's background that Schumarry found uncommon. He spoke both Mandarin and Cantonese Chinese dialects fluently, but his English was still colored with a few pidgin phrases. His college record was unblemished, though he had taken only three years of English, basic courses designed for non-native speakers, often referred to as "bonehead English." His years in the U.S. Coast

Guard, with two tours across the Pacific and Atlantic, hadn't changed that much. Paul was someone who believed in getting his message across with just a few key words, spoken or written. Physically, he was fit enough, with acceptable athletic ability, but by no means remarkable.

Less than three weeks after their introduction, Paul bravely told Schumarry he loved her. And with that, his vulnerability was revealed. At the time, he had only a few coins in his pocket. He hoped this was just a temporary condition. Their mode of transportation across Honolulu was Paul's barely running Ford Falcon convertible. Raising and lowering the canvas top was a chore, especially during a sudden downpour at the top ridge of the Pali Lookout. Their time together became more frequent. In early November 1969, Paul proposed, not in any Hollywood fashion.

He simply said, "We should get married."

Schumarry replied, "What?"

Which, in her own way, meant "yes."

Their decision to marry was made firmly and quietly, outside the knowledge of their parents.

When both sets of parents eventually learned of the engagement, their reactions couldn't have been more different. Paul's parents were happy, though some traditional questions followed. How old was she? Could she speak Chinese? They sent a scouting party to Honolulu to meet the prospective daughter-in-law, and were delighted by the report. In his heart, Paul thanked his parents for not interfering. They were simply happy that, at long last, their son had found someone he cared for.

Schumarry's parents acknowledged the news of the engagement, but remained silent during the call and for the rest of their lives. The remaining months of 1969 were quickly filled with preparations and celebratory gatherings in San Francisco. The wedding date was set for March 20, 1970. Schumarry threw herself into a whirlwind of planning to meet the fast-approaching deadline. Paul's parents and Aunt Linda helped with the logistics, securing a Bay Area location, arranging the wedding ceremony at Stanford University's Memorial Church, and selecting banquet venues between San Francisco and Palo Alto.

Schumarry's parents offered no support and stayed on the sidelines. Even so, Schumarry managed the entire wedding process on her own, gracefully navigating each setback along the way. Returning to San Francisco also meant finding a place to live. Schumarry rented a small apartment above a gas station office near the Parnassus campus. It wasn't glamorous, but it was enough.

Paul's orthopaedic residency training was structured in six-month rotations, each focused on a specific area and his personal life moved forward on a continuous path, marked by milestones, both big and small. In the middle of his third year, Paul stumbled into two life-changing moments: marriage and a confirmed acceptance into a spine fellowship training program at the University of Hong Kong's Queen Mary and Duchess of Kent Children's Hospitals.

The wedding took place at Stanford Memorial Church—formal, traditional, and closely observed by both sets of parents. After the ceremony, the newlyweds made a quick exit from the church together.

Schumarry and Paul, just after exchanging rings, stood together in the banquet hall. She wore a flowing white gown, radiant and beautiful, as the newlyweds prepared to toast their guests.

The final months of Paul's third-year residency were spent at Moffitt Hospital under Dr. William Murray's mentoring, a pioneer in joint replacements. Paul, as senior resident, assisted in all of Dr. Murray's surgeries. He requested two weeks off for his honeymoon, but Dr. Murray was not pleased. But Paul married Schumarry, and they traveled to Mexico, visiting Mexico City, Taxco, and Acapulco. While there, Schumarry endured a bout of food poisoning but still, they returned intact and joyful.

The future was still unfolding when Paul and Schumarry returned from their honeymoon. Professor Arthur Hodgson, a visiting guest from the University of Hong Kong, had arrived for a week-long exchange of orthopaedic innovations between Hong Kong and San Francisco. Professor Hodgson demonstrated anterior spine surgery techniques across all spinal levels, especially for spinal tuberculosis, an area in which he had published significant scientific papers. In exchange, the American team introduced him to advances in joint replacement surgery.

During informal conversations, Professor Hodgson mentioned he had recently established a spine fellowship program. He shared details: the program lasted one year, offered a modest stipend, and included a small apartment. Teaching would take place at the Duchess of Kent Children's Hospital and Queen Mary Hospital, with a start date of July 1, 1972.

Paul was immediately intrigued by the idea of such an exotic and specialized opportunity. Encouraged by Professor Hodgson to apply, he submitted his modest medical credentials, soon received an offer for one of the two 1972 fellowship positions. The other was awarded to Dr. Stephen Treadwell from the University of British Columbia.

Both Paul and Schumarry were involved in the decision to move to Hong Kong. Together, they agreed to accept the fellowship offer. As part of the plan, Schumarry would sit out one year of her residency training while they lived abroad. In return, Paul promised that once they returned to the United States, they would settle in the Los Angeles area, and Paul's orthopaedic practice would be based there.

The only hard reality? They didn't yet know where, exactly, in Los Angeles, that practice would be.

# 16

This was the first full year that both Schumarry and Paul worked in the same location, the San Francisco East Bay. Their respective rotations brought them to the same part of town, and life quickly settled into a routine. During this time, they had the chance to reveal deeper layers of their personalities, their values, and their perspectives on the world. Naturally, they saw things through the lens of their own lived experience, and from the vantage points of opposite genders.

Though they shared the same ethnic background, their upbringings were quite different. Schumarry was born into a prominent Manchurian family, wealthy, traditional, and steeped in rigid household protocols. Servants were part of daily life. Paul, on the other hand, was raised in a Christian Methodist home. His early years were shaped by wartime hardship and the loving care of a single mother. After the war, he was adopted by equally devoted parents. His adoptive father, a scholar from Szuchou, passed on the values of discipline, education, and quiet strength. Paul grew up without siblings and never had a close circle of friends. Despite these differences, they found ways to live peacefully with one another.

The fourth year marked Paul's role as Chief Resident. His two six-month rotations were spent in the East Bay, one at the East Bay

Children's Hospital and the other at Highland General Hospital, the county-run medical center. Some orthopaedic residents preferred to spend their senior year at the more prestigious San Francisco hospitals, but by chance, Paul's East Bay assignment ended up being a blessing. It allowed the newlyweds to avoid a year-long separation.

Prior to the tart of their East Bay training year, is another of Schumarry's important milestones, her graduation from the medical school. For the moment it was dwarfed by marriage and moving to Hong Kong. Her medical knowledge has a life long benefits.

Schumarry in her medical doctor's cap and gown, with both proud sets of parents in attendance.

Back when Schumarry was still in Hawaii completing her radiology elective, she had already secured an R-1 (internship) match at Los Angeles County General Hospital. But with Paul's fellowship in Hong Kong on the horizon and their shared desire to stay together, she canceled her L.A. commitment. Finding a new internship within the UCSF network after the official match deadline ended was no easy task. Still, Schumarry's intelligence, grace, and charm were remembered by key department chairs. With strong recommendations in hand, she was offered an R-1 internship position at Highland General Hospital without delay.

The orthopaedic residency workload at Highland was moderate, a valuable place to gain hands-on experience with common musculoskeletal injuries and diseases. While it wasn't a hub for mentorship from nationally renowned surgeons, it provided practical exposure and the space to deepen core clinical skills. Weekly didactic sessions continued at UCSF's Moffitt campus. A key expectation for senior residents was to present a project of their choosing during Saturday Grand Rounds. Paul chose to speak on "Congenital Hip Dislocation in Children," delivered in the main auditorium using slides and audio. Dr. Robert Samuelson, whom he had once mentored when both were at the same time, at Sonoma State Hospital. Dr. Samuelson was in the audience and pleased to see how far Paul had come in four years which was preceded by two years of pause to serve his Selective Service obligations.

In their first year of marriage, Paul and Schumarry discovered the quirks, both charming and challenging, of living together. Paul limited Schumarry's weekly allowance to five dollars. For his part, he had never given himself a spending allowance his entire life. On her birthday, he gave her a humorous card, but no gift. He had never expected gifts or cards for himself and assumed the same standard applied. Schumarry rebelled. She expected something more thoughtful, something tangible, and more substantial.

So, how was this "no-gift" issue resolved? They agreed to merge everything and have one set of joint bank and investment accounts. From that point forward, there would be no individual limits, no approvals needed for purchases. Each could spend as they wished, without explanation. Schumarry felt freedom and flexibility. Paul was just as content with the system. Years later, Paul could still say, "She had never cleaned out the accounts."

On weekends, they enjoyed driving to Berkeley to window shop and splurge on a good meal, usually around fifteen dollars for both.

In the final months of residency, their attention turned to preparations for their departure. They sold off most of their modest belongings. Farewell gatherings were hosted by both friends and family. A fellow resident, Robert Gilbert, bought Schumarry's Mercury Cougar coupe. Paul gave his Volkswagen to his Uncle Joseph. In hindsight, they probably should have kept both cars, they'd need them soon enough when they returned from Hong Kong.

There was also the Chairman's congratulatory party, but the best celebrations were the private parties thrown by graduating residents. At these gatherings, each graduate announced where they planned to begin their orthopaedic practice. Paul was the lone one continuing on for a year of fellowship training.

Bob Gilbert, who had purchased Schumarry's Mercury Cougar, was recruited by a prominent San Francisco group to focus on joint replacement. Rod Swarting was also headed into joint replacement, setting up practice in Twin Falls, Idaho. Three others joined traditional general orthopaedic practices, Gerome Davis and Jerry Burnhart in Walnut Creek, and Gus, who relocated to Seatle, Washington State.

The happiest of all were the residents' wives, who were already anticipating a future filled with greater income and a more luxurious lifestyle. They went nearly wild, shopping for expensive new dresses, shoes, and jewelry. The one exception was Schumarry. She knew they had at least another year of modest compensation, if any, and would continue living a down-to-earth life.

Schumarry and Paul arrived in Hong Kong for Paul's spine fellowship. At the time, the only way to cross the harbor was on the iconic Star Ferry, plans for an under-harbor tunnel were still just ideas on paper. The Star Ferry, now a symbol of Hong Kong tourism, remains a lasting image of the city's past and present.

The new spine fellow and wife travelled by taxi from Pok Fu lam Road to the front of the Queen Mary Hospital. The building structures are the primary teaching facility for the HK university School of Medicine. No excess funding was spent on the structure façade, as compared to the Harbor side business buildings.

Orthopaedic Departmental group picture in front of the Duchess of Kent Children's Hospital. Staff present include professors Hodgeson, Yau, visiting scholars, fellows, and residents.

# Part Four:

A Longevity of  Life of Love, Marriage, and Good Health in one of America's Most Glamorous Cities

# 17

Paul gave his parents thanks, in a non-verbal manner, for his life and the freedom they granted him to wander in his youth. His gestures were subtle, the kind only parents could understand, and they carried with them quiet anxieties that mothers and fathers feel but rarely voice. Their acknowledgment came in similar fashion, through presence, steadiness, and trust. The result of their upbringing shaped Paul's life: longevity in love, in marriage, in family, and in good health, from 1971 to 2025.

At the age of eighty-four, Paul began writing his autobiography. As he reflected on the years behind him, two themes emerged most vividly: the enduring strength of love and marriage, and the profound value of good health and family. These became the inspiration to record his story, in hopes that readers, too, might find similar experiences to re-capture in their own lives, their relationships, and their contributions, whether fulfilled or still unfolding.

The chapters that follow no longer adhere to a strict timeline. Life's most treasured events often emerge not in a linear fashion but in the clarity of hindsight or the stillness of memory. Paul hopes his readers might find echoes of their own experiences between these lines.

# 18

He and Schumarry had walked the same medical path, parallel yet five years apart in graduation dates from the same school. Both had been selected through a demanding admissions process that required discipline, resilience, goal-oriented focus, and the kind of intellect, real or projected, that would earn trust in exam rooms and hospital wards. They also shared the immigrant experience, each having arrived in the United States at a young age, Paul at eleven, Schumarry at eight, both learning a new language, a new culture, and how to navigate a life far from their birthplaces.

It began in Honolulu, at Queen's Hospital, with a glance, brief, casual, and yet enough to stir a feeling that the stranger across the elevator doorway was somehow…different. Paul knew nothing about her. His social world was narrow, uneventful. Outside of a polite introduction to a University of Hawaii freshman who had shown some interest, Paul's calendar was blank. In contrast, hers was not. Schumarry was already well-known in transpacific Asian circles, her title as Miss Chinatown Los Angeles trailing her like a comet tail across communities in California and Honolulu. News of her upcoming externship at Queen's had already traveled. By the time their eyes met for the first time, her social calendar was full. His, virtually nonexistent.

Paul's social résumé needed drastic improvement if it was ever going to match his peers. He lacked social grace. Schumarry recognized, even at first glance, that his aloofness toward strangers wasn't rude; it was the result of his upbringing and a deep disinterest in social ventures. Still, she noticed the short white coat he wore, the UCSF resident's logo stitched onto the sleeve. That small detail, and his quiet, unreadable demeanor, sparked her curiosity. There was an air of mystery about him. In her mind, it would be interesting to break through his seemingly indifferent façade, if she ever got the chance. Hopefully, she thought, his frosty social nature wasn't hardwired in his genes. Maybe, with the right medicine, it could be changed.

That same day, their next encounter was in the Queen's Hospital X-ray reading room. Schumarry and her extern mentor, Dr. Liese, were seated in front of the illuminated film boxes as he gave her a lesson in reading images. Paul walked in. Dr. Liese introduced them. From that moment on, they were strangers no longer. Fifty-four years later, and counting, love, marriage, and good health have followed, as if determined by fate.

Within three weeks of their first eye contact, Paul proposed. Schumarry's swift and affirmative response was just one expression of her decisive nature. Other signs revealed her strong character. Still, both of them needed time to process what had just unfolded between them. Their parents, on both sides, had no idea. The romance had been private, just two or three weeks old, yet already deeply rooted.

When Schumarry informed her parents of their engagement, the response was icy. To them, the announcement was like a betrayal, akin to the eldest daughter of a Manchurian warlord walking away from an arranged marriage designed for political alliance, family wealth, and territorial consolidation, complete with a negotiated dowry.

Up until Schumarry's college days at the University of Southern California, her parents had envisioned a very different son-in-law: a well-established doctor from the South Bay, independently wealthy, and capable of referring patients to her father's fledgling plastic surgery practice. But those plans collapsed beyond resuscitation when Schumarry made it clear she would marry contrary to their wishes.

By the time she was admitted to UCSF Medical School and crowned Miss L.A. Chinatown, Schumarry had already begun charting her own course. Her parents could only hope that their influence, and chosen candidate, had left a lasting impression. They were disappointed to discover that Paul, in every way, stood outside their vision of an ideal match.

The final insult, from their point of view, came when Schumarry and Paul chose to marry in Palo Alto at Stanford Memorial Church. Her parents, who lived in Torrance in Southern California, responded swiftly. They announced they would not attend the ceremony, would not assist with care for future grandchildren, even when it might be reasonably needed, and years later, it was discovered they had removed both Schumarry's name and her children's names from their will.

Despite this formal disavowal, Schumarry continued to call her parents weekly. She visited them on holidays. Their feelings remained mixed, on one hand, pride in her achievements; on the other, a refusal to acknowledge her place in the Chao family records.

Paul and Schumarry's love grew stronger, not just through words, but in the choices they made. Schumarry delayed the start of her residency by one year so she could accompany Paul to Hong Kong for his spine fellowship. In exchange for Paul's additional year of training, both agreed they would settle in Southern California once the fellowship ended. Schumarry had already secured a promise of an ENT (Ear, Nose, and Throat) residency position at L.A. County/USC Medical Center, starting after her one-year pause.

At the time, Paul had no clear idea how, or where, to establish a private orthopaedic practice in Southern California. During his final year of residency, he reached out to two former UCSF senior residents, Dr. John Sellman and Dr. Robert Lumsden. Both were now part of a small orthopaedic group practice in Santa Monica. They recommended that Paul contact Dr. John McGonigle, a well-established orthopaedic surgeon with a busy practice who appeared to be looking for an associate.

Dr. McGonigle offered Paul his first orthopaedic position in Santa Monica, starting July 1, 1972. The entire professional arrangement came together without any assistance from either set of parents.

In Hong Kong, the fellowship program provided Paul with a modest stipend and an 800-square-foot apartment. The unit had an ocean view on the quieter, back side of the colony, away from the busy harbor, perched on the hillside midway between Queen Mary's Hospital and the Duchess of Kent Children's Hospital. The apartment was conveniently located near the Pok Fu Lam Road bus stop, right in front of the hospital. We settled in.

Within three weeks of arriving in Hong Kong, Schumarry began showing signs of pregnancy, later confirmed by the Medical School's Obstetrics Chair. The following months were difficult, physically and emotionally, for her. Hong Kong was a foreign place to experience a first pregnancy, especially without any nearby family support. She rarely complained. Schumarry knew it would be unwise, and fruitless, to return to Southern California seeking forgiveness or support during the perinatal period.

Instead, the pair called Paul's parents and asked if Schumarry could return to San Francisco during the last month of her pregnancy and stay for a few months postpartum under their care. Their enthusiastic and cheerful response was a relief and deeply appreciated.

It was her first pregnancy, and the months that followed were uncomfortable and isolating. Hong Kong, while vibrant and modern, felt unfamiliar in this deeply personal chapter of life, and she had no family nearby to lean on. She voiced very few complaints. Returning to her parents in Southern California was not an option, there would be no forgiveness, no warm welcome during her pregnancy or postpartum recovery.

Instead, she and Paul turned to his parents. They called San Francisco and asked if Schumarry might return to stay with them for the final month of pregnancy and a few months after the birth. The answer came swiftly and with joy. Paul's parents welcomed the opportunity to care for their daughter-in-law and their soon-to-arrive grandchild.

Their peripartum plan was simple: Schumarry would return to San Francisco, deliver the baby, and remain with Paul's parents until a trustworthy, long-term live-in babysitter could be found. She flew back alone during her third trimester. Their healthy baby daughter, Lisa, was born at San Francisco Children's Hospital. Her grandparents waited anxiously outside the delivery room, the first to hold her in Paul's absence. He remained in Hong Kong, bound by the full-year fellowship he had committed to with Professor Arthur Hodgson at the University of Hong Kong.

Still, Paul asked if he might shorten his stay. Professor Hodgson granted him a two-month early departure, while still recognizing the fellowship as complete. In return, Paul promised to contribute to the department's research efforts, particularly a study on the treatment of severe spinal deformities in polio-affected children using the halo-pelvic distraction method, a surgical approach pioneered by Professor Jacquelin Perry, while at Rancho Los Amigos in Los Angeles. Though innovative at the time, the technique would eventually be replaced by safer and more effective methods involving pedicle screw instrumentation.

Nine years later, Paul, as the principal investigator, published a Hong Kong and Los Angeles research paper titled "*Embryogenesis and Prenatal Development of Vertebral Anomalies*," published in *Clinical Orthopaedics and Related Research* (Volume 151, 1980). The co-authors were Professors Yau and Hodgson. This research paper proposed how bony spinal malformation are formed during early pregnancy.

Prior to that, Paul published a case report of unusual congenital hip anomaly.

# 19

Schumarry and Lisa were thriving under the devoted care of Paul's parents. Two months after Lisa's birth, Paul returned from Hong Kong to reunite with his growing family. Even better news awaited him; they had found a kind and capable live-in babysitter, someone who would become a trusted part of the household for years to come.

One of the cornerstones of their marriage, quietly but powerfully, was financial trust. At that time, they had no steady income. Their only assets were the savings accumulated during their residency years and the modest salary Paul earned during his service with the U.S. Public Health Service and Coast Guard. Delayed gratification had been the rule of their youth, born of modest upbringings, and it carried into their marriage. Impulse purchases were avoided not out of discipline alone, but because they had learned, early on, to live simply and intentionally.

That mindset remained, even as their financial status gradually rose to the level of upper middle class and the inevitable gray hair began to appear. They understood that true security was built not only through income but through shared values. There was no need for outside validation, no temptation to overextend themselves, and no reliance on professional advice to manage their lives. Their trust in one another was complete.

Early on, they merged their finances, with one joint checking account; each of their names are authorized signatory on the final accounts. Later, this approach extended to their investment accounts. Lisa, meanwhile, continued to be cared for lovingly by her grandparents in San Francisco. She had not yet begun traveling with her parents as they transitioned to establishing a new life in Southern California. Fortunately, the same live-in babysitter who had become indispensable in the Bay Area was willing to join them in Los Angeles, offering continuity and comfort during the next phase of their family's journey.

It was time to get moving, literally. Paul and Schumarry both needed cars to begin this new chapter of our professional lives in Los Angeles. Paul purchased a brand-new Plymouth Duster for $2,300. Schumarry took over a Pontiac Firebird from her parents, though not as a gift; she paid $1,500 for it.

Neither vehicle was ideal. The Duster had no air conditioning and no power steering. Schumarry was unimpressed, especially when it came to wrestling with the steering wheel. Paul accepted full responsibility for the oversight. As for the Firebird, Paul later grumbled that while Schumarry had to buy her car, her four younger sisters each received theirs as gifts. Schumarry's response was pointed: "I would never trade my freedom for my siblings' pathetic lives."

# 20

While waiting to begin her ENT residency, Schumarry discovered a hidden talent: real estate. She combed the classifieds of the *Los Angeles Times*, scanning listings and spotting opportunities. She soon found the perfect starter home for us, located midway between the LA County Hospital and Paul's office in Santa Monica, and backing up to the Hillcrest Country Club. We needed help with the down payment, and both sets of parents contributed $6,000 to make the purchase possible. The home cost $60,000. Within a year, we had repaid our parents in full, neither set would accept interest.

Eighteen months later, Schumarry struck again. She found what would become our long-term home in Santa Monica, a Mediterranean-style house more than a hundred years old, perched on 526 Adelaide Drive. It stood just inside the northern edge of the city, with panoramic views of the ocean and the mountains. Paul agreed immediately. Schumarry negotiated the final price, arranged a second mortgage with the seller, and managed all the paperwork. They used the capital gains from the first house to help with the down payment and moved in shortly after.

526 Adelaide street in Santa Monica was the Tsous' home for forty ears, this 7,000-square-foot house featured ocean and mountain views, a rooftop solar panel array, and an indoor pool. The house's front façade is back drop for Schumarry, Lisa and Stephen.

Lisa and Stephen are growing up quickly. Here they are with their mother and father in front of the fireplace, part of the stately home's grand design.

It was the kind of house people dream about, majestic, timeless, and sitting on the edge of a bluff that seemed to touch the sky. At the time, it felt like their quiet secret. But a few years later, the rest of the world would discover the views, too. Outside the home were two sets of 250-plus steps of stairs, one set in wood and the second in cement construction; the health-conscious considered this their private stair masters.

Directly in front of the Tsous' former home is one of two well-known staircases, featuring 250 to 280 wooden steps. Some fitness enthusiasts prefer this staircase for its wooden construction, which offers a slightly more forgiving, elastic feel with each step.

Paul and Schumarry considered this house our long-term family base, their home for nearly forty years. Throughout those decades, Paul was the only one who never truly left the address for any extended period. Schumarry lived away for about two years while working for Aetna Insurance in Hartford, Connecticut. Later, during her three years with MedImpact, a privately owned PBM company, she stayed in a San Diego hotel from Sunday nights through Thursday.

Both of their children attended schools far from home. Their son, Stephen, spent his high school years at Phillips Academy in Andover, Massachusetts, from grades nine through twelve. Still, Lisa and Stephen were always happy to return to 526 Adelaide during school breaks.

Paul and Schumarry believed that having a recognizable, permanent family home was an essential stabilizing factor in their emotional development, especially during the fragile adolescent years. Stephen and Lisa always knew they had a place to return to, a refuge where they could be at peace, whether dealing with physical or emotional stress.

As for Paul, this was the beginning of an era marked by sweeping changes in medical practice and finances. He wasn't ready to transition into a different model of orthopaedic work, not the large, corporate-controlled practices, nor the narrow subspecialty surgical models that focused solely on sports injuries or spine procedures.

Schumarry, ever understanding and kind, recognized Paul's nature. She never interfered with his professional preferences or the scope of his practice. Instead, she gave him room, time, and space to follow his course and let his imagination lead the way.

From this point on, Paul and Schumarry began to discover each other's likes, dislikes, and deeper personality traits. Over time, they came to understand each other's peculiarities and made quiet adjustments, rather than confronting one another aggressively over every disagreement. There were certainly things they each liked and others disliked about the other, but chose patience and adaptation over friction.

# 21

Before the end of her first year in ENT residency, Schumarry declared that surgery, and ENT in particular, was not for her. She decided to leave the program, and there was no turning back. Paul showed his disappointment and irritation at her decision, but he also knew that once Schumarry made up her mind, no amount of reasoning, come hell or high water, could change it. He would have to accept it.

One question lingered in Paul's mind: Why hadn't she realized sooner that ENT or surgery wasn't a fit? Her answer surfaced slowly over the next few years. Schumarry simply didn't like the responsibility that came with caring for sick patients. Looking back, her decision to pursue ENT was heavily influenced by Dr. William Ho, a respected family friend and Harvard-trained specialist, who had helped her father launch his plastic surgery practice.

Schumarry had a solid grasp of medicine and an excellent bedside manner. She genuinely enjoyed listening to friends and family talk about their health concerns and helping them figure out next steps. In hindsight, Paul wondered whether specialties with less intense surgical demands, like dermatology, psychiatry, or emergency medicine, might have been a better fit.

In Paul's quiet assessment, Schumarry's psychomotor skills were underdeveloped, for reasons still unknown. She had a tendency to drop small kitchen utensils without noticing, and occasionally tripped over objects on the floor. What she did have, in abundance, was a gift for organization and a brilliant mind for strategy, skills that would shine later on when she entered the business side of medicine.

Paul, on the other hand, met the winds of change in the medical profession with deep skepticism. He was one of the last to abandon the collapsing structure of the old-fashioned private orthopaedic office practice. While he remained rooted in the traditional model, Schumarry took a very different path. In less than twelve years after leaving her ENT residency, she underwent a remarkable professional transformation.

Schumarry became the head of the LA County/USC Hospital trauma center, earned her board certification in Emergency Medicine, served as Associate Chief of the USC Student Health Services, and completed her Executive MBA at USC. She went on to establish USC's medical practice health plan and served as the Medical Director for the 1984 Los Angeles Olympic Games, overseeing track and field and swimming events at the USC campus. Whereas, Dr. Gerald Finerman of UCLA served as the corresponding medical director for the Westwood campus. And she didn't stop there.

In the years that followed, Schumarry held senior positions as the medical officer for Security Pacific Bank and later Bank of America in Los Angeles, served as medical director at Aetna in Hartford, Connecticut, and held the same role at MedImpact, a pharmacy benefit management company in San Diego. Between these fixed-location roles, she also worked as a business consultant for various medical organizations, including major pharmaceutical companies. Her career blended hands-on medical experience with strategic expertise in the business of medicine, making her uniquely valuable across the industry.

Despite Schumarry's frequent career changes and demanding roles, the bond between her and Paul never weakened. Their love for each other and for their children remained steady, unconditional, and enduring. As long as they live, that love continues.

Of course, having one parent needing a frequent "live away from home" arrangement was not ideal for a family with fast-growing young children. By the time their second child, Stephen, arrived, they had hired a second live-in babysitter. Paul, fortunately, didn't need to travel far; his two admitting hospitals, Santa Monica Hospital Hospital and UCLA St. John's, were within close proximity to each other and only three miles from their house. His office sat in between. At least half of the children's day-to-day care and supervision fell under Paul's watchful eye.

As they grew, the kids never missed out; nursery school drop-offs, piano and guitar lessons, Little League games, scout meetings, and birthday parties were all part of their rhythm. Paul made sure of it. The children were raised with a strong sense of respect, courtesy, morality, and humanity. They were also independent, often teaching themselves new things in their spare time.

Schumarry knew Paul could have earned significantly more if he had joined a larger orthopaedic spine practice or a big multi-specialty group. But Paul resisted. He valued having flexible time for both his family and himself. She understood and never pushed the issue. By then, Schumarry had become the family's primary breadwinner, and they could afford Paul's professional freedom. This freedom of professional selection gave Paul the chance to publish more than twenty orthopaedic research papers using only family funds and his own time. This degree of knowledge credentials allowed Paul to enter UCLA orthopaedic practice for the last ten years of his non-commercial or government orthopaedic jobs. The same knowledge base showed Paul is often selected to handle the most complicated California Worker Compensation legally and medically challenging cases, finding reasons for resolution on the issues.

When she returned from her consulting trips, sometimes after days or even weeks away, she would find the children healthy, well cared for, nourished, and on track. That brought her relief. Their relationship remained loving and strong. In a different setting, under different circumstances, things might have unfolded differently between them and the kids. But they made deliberate choices.

Paul and Schumarry planned long international family trips once Stephen was strong enough to walk a mile, whether it was a weekend getaway or part of a school vacation. The 2-3 week summer vacations abroad were especially fun and meaningful. The trips brought them together. They became a tradition. And they reminded them: love, expressed through time, presence, and shared joy, is one of the essential ingredients of a happy marriage.

# 22

The foursome family trips, especially in those early years just out of medical training, were not easy on the budget. Still, they made them happen. The very first extended trip was booked through Gateway Tours, a company based in Switzerland. It was a land tour, beginning in London and ending in Athens, and it included a high-speed hydrofoil crossing of the English Channel, an experience now replaced by the undersea tunnel. The accommodations were modest, and meals were basic, but for them, it was a milestone. Traveling together, making memories.

In contrast, after Paul's eightieth birthday, they took a far more luxurious journey, this time from Jordan to Egypt with Tauck Travel, a five-star trip on ancient lands , viewing Israel from the Jordanian bank, and floating on the Dead Sea. They even flew over the Red Sea from the port city of Aqaba to visit Abu Simbel, the majestic temple built by Ramses II. In Cairo, they stayed under the shadow of the Great Pyramid, a fitting symbol of time, family, and endurance.

Of course, not every trip was met with equal enthusiasm. One such example occurred while Schumarry was deep in her consulting work with Aetna in Hartford. Paul had booked a clockwise land tour of Spain, fourteen days of bus travel, with daily packing, unpacking, and a pace that only the most energetic traveler could love. The children and Paul managed just fine, but Schumarry, already exhausted from work, found the schedule grueling. Paul learned his lesson. From that point forward, Schumarry would choose the tours and the level of physical and cerebral stress before any bookings were confirmed. She made it clear: destination was secondary; the travel experience itself had to meet her standard of rest and ease.

Paul and Stephen, the father-son duo, made their preferences known as well. They could tolerate modest accommodations and fewer frills if it meant more history and more adventure.

Another lesson came from that same Spain trip. Paul had purchased Continental Airlines tickets on the grey market, from Newark to Madrid. They boarded, the doors closed, and the bridge pulled away, and the plan started to taxi. But before takeoff, a gate agent discovered the ticket discrepancy and brought the plane back to the gate. They were given a choice: to deplane or pay the full fare. They paid the fare on the spot. There was a schedule to keep, and Paul wasn't about to miss meeting Schumarry in Madrid.

During the period when Schumarry was consulting full-time and often away from home for days or weeks at a time, one might wonder whether the children were at risk for emotional instability. In hindsight, the answer is no. The steady presence of the Santa Monica home, unchanged for thirty-eight years, served as an anchor. It was a constant, a place where Lisa and Stephen always knew they could return, where they felt safe, catered, and cared for.

# 23

For the children, parental help, when needed, was quietly offered without prompting. Lisa, as a child, was notably shy and tended to avoid social interaction with her peers. Schumarry took time to speak with her gently and often, never in a forceful way. Their mother-daughter conversations continued even into adulthood, long after Lisa graduated from Columbia Law School. Over the years, Lisa's quiet demeanor evolved into the confident style of an attorney.

Stephen, on the other hand, was naturally social. He could speak with anyone about nearly anything. Paul sometimes suspected that while Stephen may not have had depth in every subject he discussed, he carried a confident grasp of many topics. In certain areas, computer science, music, and film, he went deep. That pattern revealed itself again in 2024, when Stephen became a wet lab research specialist. His work required the study of delicate, transparent zebra fish, tracing their life cycles and sensory development. It was through this process that a new kind of discipline emerged in him, one grounded in patience, technical skill, and scientific curiosity.

Of course, there were missteps along the way. But when help was needed, Paul and Schumarry provided it, quietly, without judgment, and always with love.

When Stephen began college at Carnegie Mellon University, the absence of a daily dorm floor senior supervision was inevitable. During his freshman year, he fell in love for the first time, at least, the first time his parents were aware of it, and the relationship ended abruptly. Stephen left without offering the usual parting words, and in a moment of emotional retaliation, the girl destroyed his laptop computer. Afterward, Stephen cut off communication with his parents for more than a month. Concerned, Paul flew to Pittsburgh to find him and offer support, hoping the emotional setback wouldn't leave a lasting trauma mark.

Over the next two years, Stephen embraced a more free-spirited lifestyle. He moved off campus, and his parents sent monthly checks to cover rent and living expenses. But not long after, he began cashing the checks and spending the funds without paying rent. When the landlord reached out, Paul and Schumarry stepped in to settle the balance and, from that point forward, began sending rent directly to the landlord, with a separate check to Stephen for food and pocket money.

When graduation approached, Stephen declined his parents' offer to attend the ceremony. Trusting his word, they assumed he had completed his degree requirements with his class. Over the next decade, he was occasionally asked to produce proof of his degree, requests he somehow managed to navigate. Eventually, it became clear that Stephen had not graduated. This truth surfaced when he applied for residency status in Hong Kong and couldn't provide a diploma.

Not long after the Hong Kong no university graduation diploma discovery , Stephen contacted his parents with a renewed sense of purpose. He wanted to return to Carnegie Mellon to complete the credits required for his long-deferred bachelor's degree in electrical and computer engineering. Though it had been a decade since his original class had graduated, his parents supported him without hesitation. He enrolled in an 18-month program, met the requirements, and this time, his parents were present at his graduation to celebrate his achievement.

Paul, reflecting on the moment, noted with a wry smile that he had reduced three years from high school and college studies, three years sooner than his parents had expected.

Their family home had always been one of trust, mutual respect, and wide emotional margins. Lisa and Stephen were given space to grow into themselves. Honesty, discipline, and empathy were expected, and those foundations allowed both children to develop strong, unique identities. Schumarry was never a "Tiger Mom," nor was Paul a "Dragon Dad." The children's early characteristics were only a glimpse of the depth they would reveal later in life.

Looking back, Stephen had always shown an interest in a wide range of subjects, literature, history, music, movies, sports, fashion, cars, and people. His curiosity was expansive, though not always deeply focused, with the exception of music and computer science, which Paul affectionately dubbed his son's true passions.

When asked about his graduation status after four years at Carnegie Mellon, Stephen would simply say he had "finished school." His parents, sensing he needed space, didn't press him at the time. He had an enduring love for movies and even began writing a script about a World War II concentration camp in Poland, but he couldn't bring the project to completion. The challenge of finishing what he started had long been a hurdle. Paul often remembered the advice of Dr. John Sellman from residency days: *"Finish the job at hand before moving on to another task."* That principle, passed down through experience, was one Stephen had yet to fully embrace.

Schumarry and Stephen on his graduation. Better late then never to receive diploma in computer science and electrical engineer. At the Carnegie Mellon university athletic field.

Lisa's Graduation: Lisa's undergraduate graduation from Stanford University, pictured with her grandparents, Mom and brother in front of the Stanford Memorial Church.

As Stephen drifted deeper into the creative but uncertain world of Echo Park in Los Angeles, Schumarry grew concerned. She sensed he was living without meaningful direction. Both parents suggested he pursue a business of his choosing and proposed a return to Hong Kong, where Paul's Uncle C.K. could provide mentorship and support.

Uncle C.K. had a remarkable life story, one of postwar hardship, resilience, and eventual success as a garment manufacturer. Between 1948 and 1952, Paul, Uncle C.K., and other family members had lived in a small Wai Chai apartment, surviving with little but sharing much. C.K.'s work ethic and success became a model of what perseverance could achieve.

Stephen was sent to live near the Admiralty subway station in Hong Kong, where he launched a jewelry business with his parents' financial support. For local help he had old university classmate homed in Hong Kong. For business advises seek out Grand Uncle Bernie C.K. Tung, none is better, who lives on Discovery Bay, Lantau Island HK. Stephen poured energy into the design and manufacturing of jewelry intended for export. But the business required mastery at every stage, design, production, packaging, marketing, and international sales, and Stephen soon found himself overwhelmed. The cutthroat nature of the industry, coupled with a social scene filled with expatriate distractions, left the business faltering. Despite an infusion of nearly $490,000USD from his parents, an amount matched in support previously given to Lisa, the venture never took off.

Eventually, it was time to accept the loss and begin again. Stephen returned to the U.S. quietly and made his way to Boston. He found humble work as a dishwasher in a Thai restaurant, earning enough to cover basic expenses. It was during this time that clarity returned: he needed to finish his degree. He contacted Carnegie Mellon, expressed his intention to return, and re-enrolled to complete the credits needed for a Bachelor of Science in Electrical and Computer Engineering.

After graduation, Stephen was hesitant to leap into the corporate tech world. Instead, he accepted a position at Carnegie Mellon as a teaching assistant and research contributor. Many of the research projects were conducted in collaboration with partner institutions, including Harvard Medical School. As Stephen engaged with these interuniversity teams, he began to build a reputation beyond his academic circle.

He soon discovered he could continue working on CMU-affiliated projects while living in Cambridge, Massachusetts. There, through casual encounters at the gym, pool, and bookstore, he met a principal investigator from Harvard who took an interest in Stephen's computational background. The research involved studying visual sensory input in small fish, tracking how stimuli processed through the optic nerve triggered physical reactions, all in real time. Stephen took part in handling the delicate animals and recording the data that would later contribute to groundbreaking findings.

And so, Dragon Pop offers this final piece of advice to the young researcher: If you've defined the goals of your experiment, carried it out thoughtfully, and gathered the data with care, then you're ready to begin writing the first draft. As a research assistant, Stephen now stood at that threshold. Paul suggested he take initiative and offer to draft the manuscript himself. If the study were eventually published, his name could rightfully appear second or third, just after the principal investigator.

After all the twists, turns, and detours of his academic and professional path, Stephen had come full circle.

# 24

And what of their daughter's journey? Lisa's early temperament stood in contrast to her brother's, quiet, introverted, and cautious of uncharted paths. She was deeply intelligent, with consistently high grades across her classes, but also hesitant in unfamiliar social situations. She began seventh grade at Santa Monica's public middle school and did well. But as she prepared to enter eighth grade, the school informed her that she would be placed in a combined 7th and 8th grade classroom. Half of her school year would repeat material she had already mastered.

The reasoning behind the decision was disheartening: the district had begun enrolling out-of-area students with significant special needs, and space was needed in the eighth-grade classrooms. The district's broader goals, while commendable, came at a cost to the quality of education for students like Lisa. Schumarry quickly pivoted, turning to Marlborough School, a private preparatory school located in Hancock Park, as a better fit for Lisa's academic needs.

The admissions process included an in-person interview, which posed a challenge for someone as socially reserved as Lisa. In front of the schoolmaster, she froze, answering questions in single-word replies, her expression locked in place. But Schumarry, ever the strategist, stepped in with thoughtful and persuasive explanations, helping the admissions team see the full measure of Lisa's potential. Lisa was accepted and thrived. She graduated from Marlborough with honors, a quiet but steady testament to her capability and resilience.

From her college applications, Lisa was readily accepted to Stanford University in Palo Alto. Though she also applied to several Ivy League schools, she received only waitlist notifications, a disappointment that stung. None of those waitlists cleared, as most of the top-tier spots were quickly accepted by others. Still, Stanford proved to be a strong and fitting choice. She double-majored in English and Economics, and during her second and third years, she arranged a full two-quarter exchange program at Oxford University in England, choosing to focus her studies there on English literature. By then, her parents could see how deeply comfortable and fluent she had become in both reading and writing the English language.

As her third year at Stanford came to a close, the question of a postgraduate path loomed. Her parents had no input in the matter; Lisa made her own decisions. Observing both of her parents immersed in the world of medicine, she firmly rejected it as a future career. Her decision, it seemed, was shaped more by the influence of college peers than by family example. Surrounded by conversations about liberal arts, public policy, and the occasional marvels of high tech, Lisa chose a path neither parent expected: law.

Her parents were surprised. They had missed the signals, underestimated what was taking shape in her intellectual world. At the time, Lisa hadn't yet developed the oratory confidence often associated with law students, but her performance on the LSAT told a different story.

Her score ranked in the top 0.1%, placing her in the upper echelon of applicants. She applied to a handful of Ivy League law schools and was admitted to Columbia Law School, her only offer. They suspected the more subjective elements of her application, such as recommendations and verbal communication assessments, may have tempered her chances elsewhere.

At Columbia, she found herself among an exceptionally talented group of classmates. She rose to the challenge, graduated, and made her parents proud. They attended her graduation ceremony at Lincoln Center, a moment of deep pride for the entire family. Her first job was at a New York City law firm that specialized in Initial Public Offerings (IPOs). There, the junior lawyer's role was intense: drafting public offering documents and overseeing the printing and production process. The timeline was always tight. Young attorneys were expected to live at the printer's site, reading and approving proof after proof. Lisa was no exception.

This demanding phase of her career left little time for family, and she missed several long-planned vacations. Eventually, the high-tech market crash of the 1990s led her firm to bankruptcy, and she was suddenly out of a job. She returned to Los Angeles and found work with smaller companies in need of legal counsel. By that time, she had passed both the New York and California bar exams.

At this point, Lisa realized she needed to deepen her knowledge of business law. She enrolled in the Executive MBA program at the University of Southern California, a two-year course with classes held every other weekend. The pace was demanding, but she managed it while continuing to work. The program's tuition was $60,000, but Lisa's tuition was waived as part of Schumarry's employee benefits. USC granted two years of tuition coverage for each eligible child of long-term employees or retirees. Schumarry's two decades of service opened this door for Lisa.

A key component of the EMBA program was a two-week international residency. For Lisa's cohort, the residency was held in Shanghai, China. This immersive experience allowed her to explore both foreign business regulations and the nuances of international social and professional engagement. The program introduced her to a broader network, and she began to develop the verbal and interpersonal skills essential for marketing her ideas and services.

Over the last ten years, Lisa's sharpened social abilities have helped her rise above many of her peers. Today, she works as a consultant to venture capital firms, advising them on the viability of prospective investment targets. Once a project is selected, her firm assists in drafting and reviewing the legal agreements between parties.

Has Lisa completed her circle of professional accomplishment? Yes. She began with exceptional writing skills, expanded into business through IPOs and venture capital, and now commands the verbal confidence to market her expertise.

And what of the family circle, what about happiness for the parents? Happiness, of course, is a subjective state of mind. The ingredients of long-term joy in marriage shift with time and circumstance. While marriage itself is a concept born of ancient, tribal roots, later formalized by ceremony and authority, it remains a partnership rooted in shared experience.

Sustained marital happiness requires more than love alone. Stability, emotional and physical, forms a foundation. Grown children who no longer rely on their parents for support bring another form of relief. Financial health, too, matters, achieved and maintained into the fore-seeable future.

# 25

The first decade of Paul and Schumarry's marriage was a decade of discovery, a time when their unique personalities were revealed, layer by layer. Some traits were endearing, others eccentric, and a few perhaps best tucked away. Yet even their most difficult qualities never threatened the foundation of their marriage. What follows is Paul's loving, and often humorous, list of what he admires, and what occasionally perplexes him, about his wife.

Schumarry is deeply loving, not only toward her family but toward nearly everyone she encounters. Her warmth extends to strangers with the same ease it does to close friends. She's straightforward, never hiding her emotions. And she has a remarkable memory, one that can recall, in fine detail, the financial history of a major business venture or the genealogy of the extended Chao family. However, Paul notes with a smile that her memory sometimes draws a blank on the name of a world-famous museum or where exactly the *Mona Lisa* is displayed. (Hint: It's in Paris.)

Her memory is especially sharp when it comes to topics of personal interest: clothing, jewelry, shoes, Hallmark TV series, and college or professional football. She is also an exceedingly cautious driver, so much so that Paul jokes she might be ticketed in some jurisdictions for driving *too* slowly. She does not appreciate driving advice from the passenger seat; in fact, it throws her off entirely.

Raised in a household with the trappings of Manchurian wealth and servants, Schumarry was not "house-trained" in the ways Paul was used to. She had never been expected to tighten bottle caps, turn off faucets, or pick up after herself with military precision. Paul chalked it up to her upbringing and decided it was nothing a little patient teaching couldn't fix and certainly not a reason to return her to her parents.

When immersed in a project, Schumarry tends to shut out her surroundings, what Paul affectionately calls "turning off her peripheral vision." This narrowing of focus can be both mental and physical, leading to incidents like tripping over a visible floor obstacle while rushing to answer the phone. Fortunately, she lives with a physician who's always ready to tend to minor scrapes and bumps, both physical and emotional.

Occasionally, she reacts to irritations with a quick, fiery outburst, what Paul once called "a short fuse connected to a live grenade." But just as quickly, she regains her calm, turning to logic to disarm the situation. In time, Paul jokes, he's managed to confiscate most of the fuses and grenades.

Even in the early years of their marriage, Schumarry's versatility and good sense showed through. She coordinated family logistics, offered common-sense medical advice, managed overseas fellowship travel, supported the launch of Paul's orthopaedic practice, cared for two babies from pregnancy through early childhood, and oversaw the family's major financial transactions.

And in more recent years, to Paul's great delight, she has blossomed into a truly excellent chef. With curiosity and courage, she began experimenting with various cuisines, Chinese, French, Japanese, and more. Her dishes now rival those served in Michelin-starred restaurants. In fact, Paul wonders aloud why certain simple dishes in Hong Kong receive three stars, while hers, in his view, deserve five. She said she is very allergic to porcine in any form of preparation, but is very happy to eat crispy bacon.

# 26

At the time of this writing, Paul is eighty-four years old and Schumarry is seventy-eight. They continue to enjoy each other's company, keep their minds sharp, and walk or use the treadmill three to five miles a day. They take pride in sharing the simple elements that have supported their longevity and health. Now living in Las Vegas, Nevada, they've embraced this chapter of life with grace and companionship.

Naturally, time has taken its toll on some of their organ systems. But they've been fortunate; what has declined can often be restored, either to normal or to a level of practical function, with the help of pharmaceuticals or corrective medical devices.

During medical school, Paul developed high blood pressure, likely brought on by the demands and stress of his training. After retirement, his blood pressure naturally declined to near-normal levels. With the addition of two low-cost medications, it is now consistently on the low side of normal.

He also experiences age-related vision deterioration due to a condition involving the growth of small arteries between the retinal and scleral layers (choroidal neovascularization). To prevent further loss of vision, he receives injections every eight weeks. Despite this, his vision remains functional; he recently renewed his Nevada driver's license for another four years and continues to drive, though he avoids bright lights and dimly lit environments.

Paul has moderate hearing loss, effectively corrected by a Philips hearing aid purchased from Costco. He has been fortunate to avoid common musculoskeletal issues, has no significant joint pain in his knees, hips, or hands, and has no problems with his lumbar spine.

Schumarry's primary complaints are orthopaedic in nature. She experiences tenderness and discomfort at the base of her right thumb (the metacarpal-carpal joint), which she attributes to years of chopping vegetables during home cooking. She also has mild discomfort related to her knee ligaments and patella. Common in the female gender, according to Paul, the Orthopaedist.

Her remedy? Eat out more often.

Aside from these manageable orthopaedic issues, all of her other organ systems continue to function well.

# 27

Paul and Schumarry feel deeply blessed with their continued good health and longevity. This has spared each from the worry of caring for an ailing partner, allowing them to fully enjoy their time together, whether at home or traveling.

Over the years, Schumarry came to appreciate Paul's low-key approach to traditional romantic gestures. Rather than expecting flowers or candy on special occasions, she discovered that self-procurement was often the best route. Paul, after all, is allergic to flowers, especially lilies of the valley, which cause facial swelling and upper respiratory symptoms.

She has a fondness for cashews and macadamia nuts, but avoids other varieties. Jewelry, however, remains a welcome surprise, so long as it's the right kind. While she appreciates Paul's intention, a few humorous missteps in his jewelry purchases gently nudged her toward a new strategy: choosing her pieces from a trusted jeweler in Palm Springs. Two memorable examples come to mind.

During an adventure tour to Burma with his son, Paul found himself eager to surprise Schumarry with a special gift. When their tour guide brought them to a well-regarded local jewelry shop, Paul couldn't resist the opportunity to purchase a Burmese ruby. The shopkeeper presented him with a beautiful stone at what seemed like a fair price. Paul agreed to the purchase, despite only having half the payment in cash. The shop-keeper allowed him to take the gem with a promise that the remainder would be wired to an account in Singapore once Paul returned to the United States.

Back home, Paul proudly presented the ruby to Schumarry, who promptly brought it to her trusted jeweler in Palm Springs for verification. The good news: The ruby was indeed genuine and untreated. The not-so-good news? Paul had paid more than four times its actual market value.

The second of Paul's misguided international jewelry purchases took place during a package trip to Rio de Janeiro in the 1990s. While browsing a tourist mall, he bought what he believed to be a high-quality emerald from a local merchant. Upon returning to the U.S., their trusted jeweler examined the gem and confirmed it had been treated, significantly lowering its value.

After this second misstep, Paul's days of independently shopping for jewelry came to an end. From that point forward, Schumarry handled her fine jewelry purchases. Meanwhile, the gifts from Schumarry to Paul showed no signs of slowing down.

In the 1980s, during the waning years of Paul's orthopaedic practice in Santa Monica, they decided to upgrade their image, no more unairconditioned, power-steering-less Plymouth Duster. Paul briefly drove a Mercedes 560SL convertible roadster, a stylish symbol of success. But within weeks, practicality won out. He traded the roadster for a Peugeot and a Ford Monarch, choices that did not age well. The Peugeot couldn't withstand the Arizona heat and suffered radiator-related engine damage. The Monarch began falling apart during a family trip to San Francisco: stuck windows, loose doors, and tires shedding their tread on Interstate 5.

Then came one of the most extraordinary gifts of their marriage. For Paul's 60th birthday, Schumarry organized a surprise party, gathering relatives, office partners, and colleagues from UCLA Orthopaedics. The final surprise: the keys to a brand-new Porsche 911 Carrera convertible. She had purchased it in cash, using a bonus from her work with a cousin's privately owned PBM company. The joint accounts were untouched. Paul still drives the Porsche weekly. The odometer reads just 21,000 miles.

It's a manual transmission, and both parents agreed: one of their children would inherit the Porsche someday, but only the first to learn to drive a stick shift, without grinding the gears. Paul and Schumarry even offered to fund up to four professional lessons for the contender. In the meantime, the Porsche would stay safe in a Las Vegas garage, waiting.

Paul's personality has remained steady since the beginning of their marriage. Schumarry never expected him to change. She loves him for who he is: honest, responsible, direct, a man of few words, but the right ones.

# 28

The following are a few reflections on what Paul believes his parents most treasured, expressed through quiet, non-verbal ways.

As a young man, Paul had often appeared listless and aimless during his college years. Then, seemingly out of the blue, he was accepted into two medical schools after just three years of college. It was a shock, and a point of immense, if quietly expressed, pride.

When Paul met Schumarry in Hawaii and announced they were committed to proper church marriage within four months, his parents were stunned once again. They had long wondered if Paul had any interest in romantic relationships at all, perhaps imagining he'd been too private or selective. Unbeknownst to them, Paul had encountered more than a few eligible women during his years in schools and as a sailor across two oceans.

In the last fifteen years of his and Schumarry's lives, Paul made an effort to create a sense of closeness and continuity. He asks for weekly, entire family gatherings and, along with Schumarry, has arranged live-in care for them, paid for by their children, ensuring they were surrounded by love and dignity until the end.

Uncle Bernie C.K. Tung's 91st birthday celebration, joined by Schumarry and Paul at his Siena Mansion penthouse in Discovery Bay, Hong Kong.

The Tsou family's first holiday card—simple and heartfelt—featuring a single photo from their first long family trip to Alaska.

The 2024 family holiday card, printed front and back with travel images from the previous 12 months.

The 2024 family holiday card, back side of card.

Paul at Machu Picchu, after hiking the Inca Trail for three days to reach this iconic viewpoint.

Potola is a magnificant Holy structurre for worship. It also houses the Stupas of all Dali Lamas holy remains and artifacts of the past and present, except two. The current Dalai Lama resides in India and the second Dalai Lama not represented lived more than 100 years ago and preferred wine and people of the opposite gender and therefor not elegible to be buried at the stupa.

Overnight camping experience in Antarctica, tent pitched on the ice.

The family dining in the shadow of the Great Pyramid of Giza.

Taking a dip in the Dead Sea, with a view of Israel from the Jordanian side.

In India, Schumarry ("the crazy lady") climbed an elephant and later walked to the front of the Taj Mahal.

In front of the Taj Mahal in india.

She races toward the massive red Uluru rock in Australia to pose—only to be firmly instructed, "Do not climb."

Now dressed as a Manchu princess, she poses in the Forbidden City, honoring the protocol from President Nixon's historic visit.

# Part Five:

A Lifelong Commitment to Learning

# 29

After Paul entered adulthood, his learning categories in life branched into two distinct paths. One path led him into the rigorous world of professional knowledge, the information required to care for patients and perform surgery with skill and precision, as the condition requires. The other path was for his enjoyment: subjects chosen simply for the pleasure of knowing. In this next section, Paul will share the story of his long journey through spine surgery education, repeated briefly, as well as his personal philosophy on how one ought to pursue a professional life of education in medicine.

Paul stood at both the edges and the very center of academic medicine for nearly five decades. For Paul's first thirty years after his spine fellowship, he served as a voluntary, unpaid instructor in orthopaedics. In the final decade of his career, he re-joined the faculty at UCLA as a paid full-time staff orthopaedic surgeon. His last twelve years brought a new focus: mastering the complexities of California's state worker injury impairment compensation within the medical-legal framework.

Paul's perspective on education in orthopaedic spine surgery begins with this: start with a broad and solid curriculum. Do not rush to specialize before understanding the pertinent disease pathogenesis in depth. Seek out every opportunity to learn. Take no shortcuts. Understand the "why" before the "how." That, in Paul's view, is the only way to practice with confidence, integrity, and skill.

Paul entered private practice in orthopaedics in the early 1970s, at the very edge of what would become the most transformative period in modern medicine. Over the decades that followed, he would witness sweeping changes in nearly every corner of the profession: the evolving nature of the doctor-patient relationship, the tightening grip of medical economics and reimbursement by large medical corporations and the government, the flood of over priced but not necessarily better new pharmaceuticals and surgical devices, the rise of advanced technologies, and the unimaginable inflation of healthcare costs.

At the time, while still completing his orthopaedic spine fellowship in Hong Kong, Paul had no clear picture of what his professional future would look like, only one certainty: his practice must be based in Southern California. This had been his promise to Schumarry, and he meant to keep it.

Timely help came from two of Paul's former UCSF senior residents, Dr. John Sellman and Dr. Robert Lumsden. They had already established themselves in a four-person group practice in Santa Monica and in no need of a new associate. They introduced Paul to Dr John McGonigle, who is the busiest orthopaedic surgeon in West Los Angeles.

Paul and Schumarry met Dr. McGonigle at a Holiday Inn just off Los Angeles's 405 freeway and Sunset Boulevard. Dr. McGonigle was physically imposing, nearly three hundred pounds, but warm, likeable, and quick to laugh. Dr. McGonigle read Paul's residency and fellowship training history. Without hesitation, he offered Paul a job on the spot. The salary: $40,000 per year, an extraordinary offer for someone freshly out of training. Paul accepted. It was the start of a new chapter.

Here is Paul's firsthand account of the tightly-knit and fiercely territorial, and competitive orthopaedic landscape he entered upon arriving in Santa Monica. The practice used two local hospitals: St. John's Hospital, operated by the Sisters of Charity of Leavenworth, Missouri, and Santa Monica Hospital, which was under the ownership of the Methodist Church medical system, which in early 1990s absorbed into the UCLA Health systems. Santa Monica Hospital/UCLA has the capability to care for a wide spectrum of illnesses, except will refer major trauma victims, just taken off the busy US Highways 405 and 10 and other freeways, to the Ronald Reagan UCLA Hospital in Westwood. St. John's maintained a "closed" emergency department, only accepting patients referred by physicians already on staff, while Santa Monica Hospital still retained a county-certified active emergency room and was open to general admissions.

It was no easy feat to gain staff privileges at either institution. Admission often required personal sponsorship from an established physician within the hospital ranks. Paul was fortunate to be "rubber-stamped" into associate membership at both hospitals, thanks to Dr. McGonigle's endorsement. Still, the quiet undercurrent of institutional discrimination remained evident, even in the mid-twentieth century.

Paul's practice schedule was intense from the outset. He saw patients in the office one full day and two half days per week, often up to fifty in a full day. He also rotated through emergency room call duty and maintained two surgical days each week. Those surgical days were reliably full of operative cases. Remarkably, John McGonigle allowed Paul to handle all surgical cases independently, but John was always the surgeon of record in the final operative report. A significant portion of the practice consisted of personal injury and workers' compensation cases, in addition to general orthopaedics and a high volume of lumbar spine fusions.

John's method of spine surgery followed a consistent, and somewhat theatrical, pattern. Each lumbar fusion began with co-surgeon Dr. William Dodge, a neurosurgeon formerly of the Mayo Clinic, who would enter the operating room, remove the disc, and promptly exit. Then, Dr. McGonigle and his team took over to perform the posterior H-shaped bone graft fusion. The graft, named for its shape, was wedged between two spinous processes, forcing the spine into a flexed position. Paul noted that while technically effective, this technique reduced the natural lordosis of the lumbar spine, a compromise with long-term implications.

Outside of the operating room, John maintained an extravagant lifestyle. He hosted an elaborate Christmas party each year at his gated estate in Pacific Palisades, where guests, including Paul and Schumarry, were treated to lavish food, ornate decorations, and the presence of Mrs. McGonigle, covered in expensive jewelry. The couple had twelve children. Despite his full medical schedule, John also managed a sprawling business empire outside of medicine.

Not long after that first Christmas holiday party, John surprised everyone. He divorced his wife of more than forty years and married Vi, a radiology technician in her thirties. Soon after, the newlyweds left Santa Monica for a quiet life on a farm nestled in the Sierra foothills. It was as if John had simply reached his limit with the relentless pace of life in coastal California and decided to begin again.

The heavy demands of a busy orthopaedic practice had begun to take a toll, physically and mentally, on Paul. With each passing day, the idea of leaving Dr. McGonigle's office grew more certain. In the early spring of that year, two significant events hastened the unraveling. The first was tragic: the most senior and respected partner in Dr. Sellman's group, an accomplished surgeon from a wealthy family, known for his research contributions, took his own life in the office. The second was quieter but no less impactful: Dr. Robert Lumsden divorced his wife and wealth and relocated to Longmont, Colorado, marking another departure from the original practice circle.

Paul first sent his formal letter of resignation directly to Dr. McGonigle. He offered to remain for one month to allow time for a replacement to be found. However, upon receiving the letter, Dr. McGonigle responded curtly: "You can leave now. Give me your office keys and clear your desk." The office locks were changed that same day.

The abruptness of the encounter left Paul momentarily stunned. When he relayed what had happened to Drs. John Sellman and Ted Lynn, they immediately invited him to join their office that very same day.

Dr. Ted Lynn, a distinguished orthopaedic surgeon in his own right, was a World War II veteran who had trained at New York's Hospital for Special Surgery. Known as much for his surgical expertise as for his artistic side, Dr. Lynn was divorced and an accomplished cellist, living with a 30-something-year-old lady fellow cello player.

The new office was formed: Lynn, Sellman & Tsou Orthopaedic Specialists, Inc., located at 2001 Santa Monica Boulevard. The address had a legacy, descended from a long-established practice. It attracted few medico-legal cases but held a patient list filled with notable names from the entertainment industry, Reagan, Taylor, Madden, The Beach Boys, and others.

# 30

*The following is a list of Paul's lifelong learning experiences, not necessarily in chronological order, but each one marked by Paul as a significant unforgetable learning event. The details learned is either highly valuable for ever or should only be send to the archive, stat.*

# 31

## Information: Useful Now Or Immediately Destined For Archive Storage.

The following section contains Paul's reflections on the comprehensive spine knowledge he acquired over several decades of medical practice. His journey into the complexities of spinal care was not limited to one anatomical region, cervical, thoracic, or lumbar, but evolved organically, shaped by patient need, clinical curiosity, and the full spectrum of musculoskeletal disorders he encountered in both academic and private settings.

Some of what follows may be inspiring, encounters with mentors, cases that affirmed his instincts, or innovations that improved outcomes. Others may reveal the limitations of prevailing practices when well-intended methods lack the necessary scientific grounding or logical coherence. Paul's professional path did not take the narrow route of many modern specialists who limit themselves to a single joint or surgical technique. His was a broader practice, rooted in general orthopaedics, seasoned by real-world complexity, and informed by adjacent pathologies that often presented alongside more urgent musculoskeletal issues.

In today's medical landscape, it is not uncommon for orthopaedic colleagues to focus exclusively on one corner of the field. Spine surgeons may operate only on lumbar discs, joint specialists may confine themselves to knees and hips, and sports medicine doctors may hone in on ligament repair. Yet even for these highly focused practitioners, Paul would advocate: keep the lens wide. Refresh general medical knowledge. Remember, the body is an interconnected system. It is in this spirit that the following insights are offered, not as prescriptions, but as a record of learning, trial, observation, and ongoing curiosity.

## Deep Spine Knowledge: Learn It Fully And Question The Significance Of The Trends.

In spine surgery, techniques come and go, often marketed with great enthusiasm, sometimes backed by science, other times simply riding a wave of popularity. Paul learned early on: what is fashionable in the operating room today may be discarded tomorrow. High-tech devices and elaborate procedures often arrive with promise, but only time reveals their true worth. Longevity in practice demands discernment.

## Write To Document As A Lifelong Companion

Paul's first meaningful encounter with complex spinal deformity occurred during his earliest days as a first-year resident at Sonoma State Hospital. The children there, many with cerebral palsy or neurologic conditions, often suffered from severe spinal curvatures. His mentor, Dr. Robert Samuelson, focused more on hip dislocations than spines, but he taught Paul something even more lasting: how to design a clinical research project and how to write a document for publication. That process, thinking critically, gathering evidence, and communicating findings, became a lifelong companion. Writing research papers was not just an academic exercise; it was a tool for deeper understanding and a way to contribute to the collective medical body of knowledge.

## Hold On To The Basics

Paul never let go of the foundational knowledge that shaped him. One of the early didactic assignments during his residency was on the embryological development of the nervous system, from brain to peripheral nerves. He learned how neural crest cells give rise to the central and peripheral nervous systems long before any organs are formed. That information stayed with him. Decades later, he authored two basic science papers rooted in those early lessons:

# Embryogenesis and Prenatal Development of Congenital Vertebral Anomalies and their Classification

PAUL M. TSOU, M.D., ARTHUR YAU, F.R.C.S.,* AND A. R. HODGSON, F.R.C.S.**

From the Duchess of Kent Children's Orthopaedic Hospital, Hong Kong, and The Orthopaedic Hospital, Los Angeles, California.
Reprint requests to Paul M. Tsou, M.D., 2001 Santa Monica Boulevard, Santa Monica, CA 90404.
Received: September 21, 1979.

0009-921X/80/1000/211 $01.55 © J. B. Lippincott Co.

211

"Embryogenesis and Prenatal Development of Congenital Vertebral Anomalies and Their Classification" — published in Clinical Orthopaedics and Related Research, 1980.

That early curiosity, paired with careful instruction, became a reservoir of knowledge that supported him throughout his career.

## Keep the Channels Open Across Time and Across Generations

In 2025, Paul finds himself 84 years old, in conversation with his son Stephen, now a biomedical researcher at Harvard Medical School. One of Stephen's research projects involves studying the zebra fish's optic nerve's electrical activity, how it transmits signals to the brain, and the behaviors that result in live experimental models. For Paul, the ability to discuss these topics across generations is a profound joy. Though the tools have changed, what once required weeks of lab work now happens in real-time, with advanced imaging and AI-enhanced analysis, the heart of the work remains the same: curiosity, observation, and a drive to understand the body in motion and in rest.

The lesson? Stay grounded in basic science. Keep writing. And most importantly, keep the lines of communication open with your students, your colleagues, and your children. Whether by phone, by paper, or face to face, keep talking. Keep listening.

## Keeper of the Old Wisdom: The Traditional Manometer and Vertebral Disc Pressure Data

In the early days of Paul's training, the clinical management of spinal conditions, especially surgical intervention, was not a strength of the UCSF Orthopaedic Department. That territory belonged, by tradition and turf, to the Department of Neurosurgery. What Orthopaedics at UCSF *did* offer, however, was world-class spine biomechanics research.

One of the department's most notable contributions came from Dr. James and a visiting Swedish postdoctoral researcher, Dr. Alf Nachemson. Together, they conducted a groundbreaking study that captured the attention of the spine world. Using brave volunteer subjects, they inserted fine needles directly into the lumbar discs, which were connected to pressure manometers that recorded real-time, in vivo disc pressures during different body positions.

The results were eye-opening.

Sitting upright produced the *highest* pressure readings within the lumbar discs. In contrast, lying on one's back with the hips and knees gently flexed produced the *lowest*. Their data upended popular ideas at the time, particularly those promoted by a New Zealand exercise expert who championed aggressive lumbar extension exercises as a universal cure for back pain.

The research underscored a critical truth: not all movements are therapeutic for all spines. And empirical data, not dogma, must guide clinical decision-making. Paul remembered this well. It was a keeper.

## Technique Before Knowledge: A Lesson Best Stays Dormant In The Archives

Early in his career as a spine attending at UCLA, Paul faced a case that would mark him deeply. A young Japanese national patient arrived at the spine clinic with a severe, fixed cervical extension deformity. All available diagnostic studies of the time were completed. Paul, believing he had identified a solution, proceeded with surgery.

The plan was to remove the posterior tethering structures, those anatomical restraints preventing the neck from returning to a more functional, neutral position. The surgery was carried out under Paul's supervision.

That night, the young man died.

Paul accepted responsibility. He had not done the research to understand the broader biomedical implications of the patient's condition. He had approached the case as a mechanical problem to be fixed with a mechanical solution. What he failed to recognize, which had not yet entered the spine literature in a meaningful way, was that the patient likely suffered from a rare condition later found to be associated with central sleep apnea, a disorder in which the brain fails to send the proper signals to maintain breathing during sleep.

Neither Paul nor his team was prepared for this. The surgery removed the tethers, but the danger was not in the neck's fixation. It was in the brainstem's silence. This loss still echoes.

## New Techniques in the Wrong Setting: When Profit Clouds Judgment

By the 1970s, spinal deformity surgeries became more common, and with them came a surge in intraoperative spinal cord monitoring. Electrodiagnostic studies, those involving proximal stimulation and distal signal recording, offered surgeons real-time insight into spinal cord function during high-risk corrections. These signals became invaluable. When warning signs arose, the surgeon could pause, reassess, and prevent injury.

But as the technology advanced, so did its misuse.

Paul watched with concern as some practitioners began applying intraoperative monitoring to surgeries that did not involve the spinal cord at all, such as peripheral nerve procedures related to work injuries. The justification? A vague assertion that long-term peripheral nerve damage had been discovered in cases of fractures and dislocations.

To Paul, this logic was flawed. Yes, nerve injuries can occur in complex trauma. But in those instances, clear visualization and proper reduction techniques were the true safeguards, not unnecessary and costly monitoring. Using high-level diagnostic tools in low-risk scenarios served one purpose: financial gain. Science didn't support it, and anatomy didn't require it.

Years later, when Paul took on medical-legal review in the California workers' compensation system, his clear grasp of both anatomy and appropriate technology lent weight to his opinions. He knew the difference between care and overreach. And he remembered the importance of humility, learned the hard way, in a quiet hospital room, long ago.

### Knowing More To Avoid Pitfalls: Select The Spine Anterior Approaches for the appropriate pathology

Paul's spine fellowship in Hong Kong proved to be one of the most formative chapters of his professional education. It offered not only an expansion of technical skill but also a window into a different global approach to spinal surgery, particularly anterior access to the thoracic and lumbar spine.

In North America, this anterior approach had long been considered the territory of general surgeons. Because they were already trained in navigating the intraperitoneal and retroperitoneal spaces, orthopaedic surgeons were often relegated to the posterior spine. Medico-legal boundaries and training structures limited U.S. orthopaedists' exposure to the front side of the spine. In contrast, British and Commonwealth systems, such as those in the U.K., Canada, and parts of Asia, required that all surgeons first become Fellows of the Royal College of Surgeons, or the national equivalent, before pursuing subspecialty training in fields like orthopaedics or urology. This foundational training allowed them to move more freely between surgical territories.

In Hong Kong, Paul learned the techniques and risks associated with anterior spinal access, knowledge rarely taught to his American peers. He witnessed firsthand the use of the halo-pelvic traction method to correct spinal curvatures in children with polio, a technique developed at Rancho Los Amigos in Los Angeles by Dr. Jacquelyn White. Though innovative at the time, Paul came to believe it should never have been applied to human subjects. The method relied on the placement of pins into the iliac crests, with a rigid pelvic ring to apply longitudinal distraction. But in patients with certain pelvic anatomies, particularly a deeper iliac concavity, these pins could traverse into the peritoneal sac, risking colon perforation. A few tragic outcomes revealed the inherent danger. The lesson: understanding anatomy is not optional.

## Use a Handful of Pedicle Screws to Stabilize Major Spine After Major Spine Trauma and Deformities.

In contrast to this, newer, safer methods were emerging. Dr. Suh of South Korea introduced a technique that would ultimately change the field: pedicle screw fixation for spinal deformity correction. Unlike earlier techniques that relied on distraction to straighten curves, Dr. Suh's approach used pedicle screws inserted directly into the vertebral bodies and corrected the deformity with direct manual pressure. Two parallel rods stabilized the realigned spine. Paul was among a small group of scoliosis surgeons invited to witness the procedure in Seoul. Incredibly, Dr. Suh placed all screws by hand, without fluoroscopic guidance, demonstrating both precision and deep anatomical knowledge. Paul's education didn't end there.

In the rising era of minimally invasive spine surgery, he expanded his skill set further, learning from pioneers like Dr. Tony Yeung in Phoenix, Arizona. Dr. Yeung developed a technique using the Holmium: YAG laser to reach previously inaccessible areas of the lumbar spine through a posterolateral approach. The procedure required only a one-centimeter skin incision, with a working channel guided by fluoroscopy to the target disc. A high-resolution scope with a 30-degree viewing angle provided a clear visual field, while continuous saline irrigation protected surrounding tissues from thermal injury during laser ablation.

The true advancement, however, came from the laser's ability to fire laterally. For the first time, the surgeon could reach the lateral recess and foramen without removing large portions of bone. Instruments passed through separate channels in the tube, one at a time, each action performed under direct visualization. This method allowed for safe and effective decompression of nerve roots, all with minimal disruption.

In Paul's mind this technique has not yet reached it's full potential. Dr. Yeung is an excellent surgeon using the minimally invasive method using the laser, scope and special tools. He is not a scientific research writer who can write papers to propagate the new method.

In 2005, Paul patented his method for a minimally invasive postero-lateral approach to the lumbar spine, an innovative technique he first introduced through a peer-reviewed article and detailed illustrations, pioneering the use of the Holmium YAG laser in tight surgical spaces, despite its steep learning curve and high equipment cost.

(12) **United States Patent**      (10) **Patent No.:**    **US 6,851,430 B2**
Tsou      (45) **Date of Patent:**     **Feb. 8, 2005**

(54) **METHOD AND APPARATUS FOR ENDOSCOPIC SPINAL SURGERY**

(76) Inventor: **Paul M. Tsou**, 2001 Santa Monica Blvd., Suite 1190 W., Santa Monica, CA (US) 90404

( * ) Notice: Subject to any disclaimer, the term of this patent is extended or adjusted under 35 U.S.C. 154(b) by 0 days.

(21) Appl. No.: **09/997,361**

(22) Filed: **Nov. 30, 2001**

(65) **Prior Publication Data**

US 2002/0077632 A1 Jun. 20, 2002

**Related U.S. Application Data**

(60) Provisional application No. 60/333,038, filed on Nov. 16, 2001.

(51) Int. Cl.⁷ .................. **A61B 19/00**; A61B 17/32
(52) U.S. Cl. .......................... **128/898**; 606/79; 606/86
(58) Field of Search ........................... 606/79; 128/898

(56) **References Cited**

U.S. PATENT DOCUMENTS

| | | |
|---|---|---|
| 4,545,374 A | 10/1985 | Jacobson |
| 5,501,654 A | 3/1996 | Failla et al. |
| 5,792,044 A | 8/1998 | Foley et al. |
| 5,902,231 A | 5/1999 | Foley et al. |
| 6,217,509 B1 | 4/2001 | Foley et al. |
| 6,261,311 B1 | 7/2001 | Sharkey et al. |
| 6,270,498 B1 | 8/2001 | Michelson |

OTHER PUBLICATIONS

[Author not identified], "Posterior 4022 Paddle Tube Surgical Technique BAK Lumbaar Interbody Fusion System;" Brochure Copyright 1999, 23 pages, published by Sulzer Medica, Minneapolis, MN 55439–2027, U. S. A.

Primary Examiner—Cary E. O'Connor
Assistant Examiner—Candice C. Stokes
(74) Attorney, Agent, or Firm—Kleinberg & Lerner, LLP

(57) **ABSTRACT**

A method of performing percutaneous transforaminal endoscopic lumbar surgery on a patient, includes the steps of creating an opening in the patient's skin, passing at least one tubular cannula through the opening so as to create a soft tissue tunnel, placing a semi-tubular spreader over the at least one tubular cannula inside the soft tissue tunnel, placing a flat blade spreader into an opening formed by the semi-tubular spreader, dilating the opening by spreading apart blades of the flat blade spreader, inserting bone grafts through the opening and into an intervertebral space of the patient.

**16 Claims, 11 Drawing Sheets**

U.S. Patent #6,851,430 B2, issued on February 8, 2005

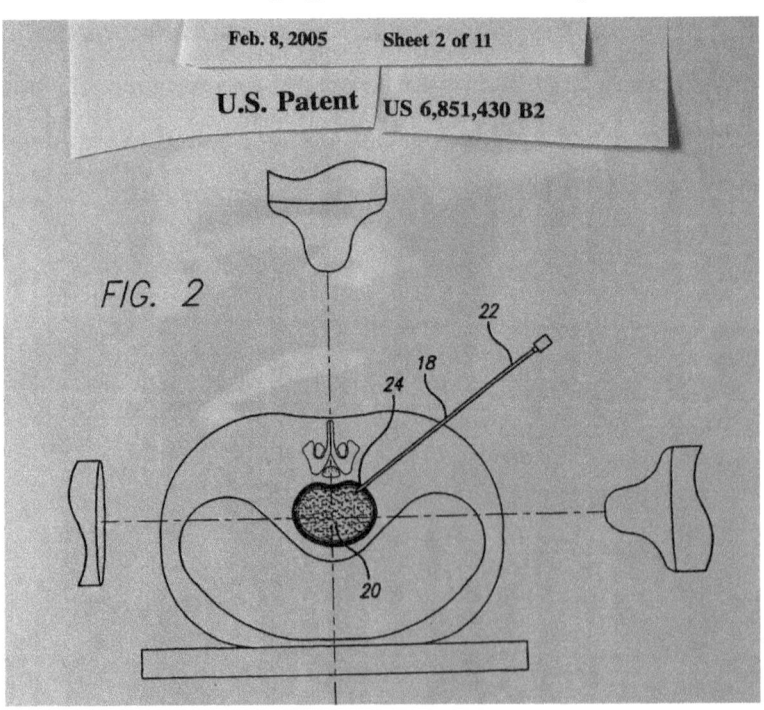

Surgical setup using two or more planes of X-ray fluoroscopy.

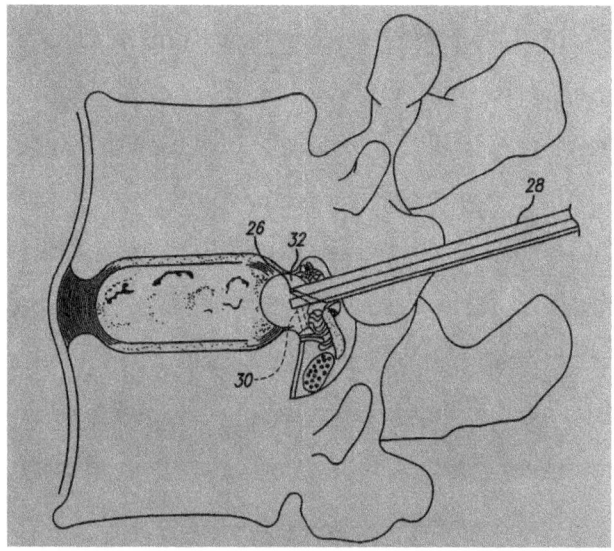

Cross-sectional view demonstrating how the minimally invasive tool operates beneath the transverse process and within the intervertebral disc space; Holmium YAG laser shown as the cutting and ablation instrument.

Paul believed this approach might one day serve as the delivery pathway for future biologics, stem cells, targeted drugs, or other regenerative agents, directly into the anterior vertebral column.

The enduring lesson? Knowledge must precede technique. Always.

## Stem Cells Clinical Usage : Still Waiting To Be Awakened

The phrase "stem cells" continues to evoke wonder and expectation, yet also a measure of disappointment. The scientific community is still waiting to unlock the specific genetic code that will guide undifferentiated stem cells into mature, fully functioning tissue types: bone, nerve, muscle, islet cells, and other organ-specific derivatives.

In Paul's era of spine surgery, he observed how early enthusiasm often outpaced results. Industrial giants had already entered the arena, hopeful that stem cell-rich aspirates might improve surgical outcomes.

At high-volume centers like St. John's Hospital in Santa Monica and at UCLA, it became common practice to harvest iliac crest aspirate during spine fusion surgeries, mixing it with autologous or donor bone, sometimes adding platelets, then placing this mixture at the fusion site. The hope was that such a biological cocktail would boost fusion rates.

But results fell short of expectations. Clinical studies did not demonstrate significant improvements in outcomes using these so-called "stem cell-enriched" techniques. Paul suspects the failure lies not in the concept, but in the missing genetic activator, the elusive endogenous trigger that awakens primordial cells and steers them toward a specific, functional lineage. Until that key is discovered in the genetic laboratory, stem cells remain a promise not yet fulfilled.

## The Enduring Value Of Clinical Research

Despite its modest reputation compared to basic science or biotech innovation, clinical research remains a vital part of modern medicine. Paul saw its value firsthand, both in large academic institutions and in community-based studies. With a sufficient number of cases, statistical analysis can illuminate which treatment protocols provide the most reliable results for specific patient populations.

During his final decade of practice, Paul worked as a full-time orthopaedic surgeon at UCLA. In those years, he authored and published three research papers related to spinal care. Two focused on trauma, one involving the lumbosacral spine and the other the cervical spine. A third paper explored the significance of measuring the anteroposterior diameter of the lumbar spinal canal.

That last study had lasting clinical implications. Understanding the natural variation in spinal canal dimensions is crucial when evaluating disc herniations or stenosis. A smaller, congenitally narrow canal with the same volume of intrusion will have a greater percentage of space compromised, information that directly affects surgical decision-making. Though some institutions use total cross-sectional area to evaluate canal size, Paul's research found the simple anteroposterior measurement both practical and predictive.

## The Cost Of Clinical Research

The beauty of clinical research is that its cost, at least in its purest form, is relatively low. A dedicated researcher needs little more than a clear study design, institutional approval, access to well-documented medical records, a laptop, Microsoft Word, and a reliable pen. Time and persistence are the greatest investments.

Paul's own published studies, roughly 85 percent, were derived from chart reviews at major hospitals or UCLA. The remaining 15 percent involved collaborative projects where he served as a contributing investigator. These efforts cost him nothing beyond his own time, energy, and attention to detail.

That said, not all research is so economical. Product-driven clinical trials, especially those involving new devices, often require budgets in the hundreds of thousands, sometimes millions, of dollars. Paul once engaged with a major device manufacturer interested in laser-assisted ablation for herniated lumbar discs. After initial exploration, the company shifted focus, choosing instead to invest in a European-designed artificial lumbar disc. The outcome was unfortunate. The disc implant proved unreliable, with high failure rates and complex revision surgeries. The project ultimately cost the company hundreds of millions of dollars.

Paul's conclusion? Sometimes the best research is the kind driven by curiosity, not capital. It might not cost much, but it can save much more.

## Step Into The World Of Workers' Compensation. A specific type of Medicine: California Style

After retiring from his full-time orthopaedic role at UCLA, Paul chose not to step away from medicine entirely. Instead, he stepped into a new role, one requiring more discernment than dexterity: that of a Panel Qualified Medical Examiner (QME) within California's Department of Workers' Compensation. He limited himself to 2–4 days of work per month and made a conscious decision to accept only panel cases appointed directly by the state. No private referrals, no lobbying for work, only impartial review.

These panel cases often involved attorneys on both sides and nearly always contained unresolved disputes. Frequently, they centered around complex patients, individuals with significant preexisting conditions: cancer, diabetes, renal failure, obesity, and prior injuries, all of which needed to be considered. In workers' compensation medicine, this process is called *apportionment*, the allocation of responsibility for a patient's impairment. What portion of the disability is due to the work injury, and what portion stems from non-work-related factors?

Apportionment can range from 100% industrial to 100% non-industrial. And unless the QME has deep knowledge of both general medicine and orthopaedics, the judgment rendered can be lopsided, unfair to one side or the other.

Paul quickly recognized the fault lines in the system. Employers and insurers are reluctant to acknowledge an injury unless there's dramatic evidence, "dripping blood or protruding bone," as he put it. Many soft tissue injuries or chronic strain conditions are met with skepticism. Delays in approval lead to delays in treatment. Deterioration follows. Meanwhile, some injured workers, directed by attorneys, end up in underqualified treatment networks offering excessive or irrelevant care. Another flaw: both parties must agree on which medical records the QME receives. This negotiation often dilutes the full clinical picture.

The system, by design, is no-fault. But in practice, it is expensive, inefficient, and often ineffective. Paul observed that the truly injured worker, one who has suffered a legitimate and often debilitating injury, may receive only a fraction of the total cost spent in their name. Legal fees, administrative costs, and dubious treatments consume most of the budget.

In contrast, Paul and Schumarry now find joy in a simpler kind of medicine. They offer free advice to friends and family, no billing codes, and no legal forms. Just help. Just healing. They've eased anxieties, prevented unnecessary surgeries, and saved more than a few loved ones from expensive or ineffective treatments.

It's satisfying to return to the roots of medicine: good history-taking, thorough physical examination, clinical reasoning born of decades of experience. The lessons learned over fifty years ago in medical school remain relevant. Sometimes, even now, the best diagnostic tools are the simplest: attentive listening, compassionate curiosity, and the ability to tell what's real pain, and what's not, without ever ordering a test.

# EPILOGUE
## A Life in Full

As the final pages of this story are written, Paul sits not at a hospital desk, nor at a conference table, but at home, a lifetime behind him. He is no longer in surgery, no longer fielding pages or reviewing scans. Instead, he is reviewing something more intricate: the long, textured map of a life built from discipline, duty, and devotion.

This memoir is not a declaration of perfection. It is a record of perseverance. It is the quiet recollection of a man who, against the odds, made a meaningful life, both in the operating room and around the family table. From orphaned beginnings in wartime China to academic hallways in San Francisco and operating suites in Santa Monica, Paul's journey has been marked by transformation and quiet resolve. In looking back, he sees that the sum of his life's experience has left him with a certain measure of wisdom, one he offers now to the younger generations who come to this land of freedom and possibility, where the doors are many and the chance to rise is real.

And yet, the most enduring accomplishments of Paul are not the surgeries performed or the titles earned, but the relationships sustained. A marriage that began with a glance in a Honolulu hospital and turned into more than fifty years of partnership. Two children, raised with care, each carving their own path. And a devotion to medicine that was never about prestige, but about usefulness. About showing up. About doing the job well and letting that be enough. In the same realm, I pay tribute to the few schoolmates from UCSF who devoted their entire professional lives to patients who needed health care and comfort. They live in less comfortable and sometimes even on dangerous grounds without asking for reasonable material comfort in return. These classmates each made their mark, contributing in their own way to the betterment of the world they lived in.

My goal and hope are simple: to explore how we can make America a better place. This can be done through words that inspire and sweat that builds. These are the principles I believe in and strive to live by. I hope you will carry them forward. I hope, the ideals will solidify in the mind of those who also want to make America a better place.

- Truth
- Honesty
- Character
- Respect your parents, seniors and teachers
- Be faithful to your spouse
- Keep promises given and kept
- Wealth is earned
- Gift only that you have earned by your own sweat
- Valor and bravery are earned
- Diligence exceeds expectation
- Advertise not your own achievements
- Be tolerant of reasonable differences

While writing this autobiography, I came across my naturalization document, the one that made me a citizen of the United States of America. With it, I pledged my allegiance and loyalty to this country. In truth, I believe I have received far more from this land than I have given during my lifetime under its flag. But I am not done yet. There is still time, and still work to do.

Now, in the years of reflection, Paul and Schumarry live in quiet companionship. Their walks are slower, but still purposeful. Their minds still sharp, their conversations still full of curiosity and laughter. They are no longer racing toward anything. Instead, they are making space for memory, for presence, and for grace.

If there is one message this book leaves behind, it is this: A well-lived life is not made from brilliance alone, but from steadfastness. From showing up when no one is watching. From knowing what matters most and tending to it carefully, again and again.

Medicine gave Paul a career. Schumarry gave him a home. And together, they made a family. This, above all, is the legacy worth writing down.

—Paul M. Tsou, MD
Las Vegas, Nevada
2025

# Biography

Dr. Paul "Moody" Tsou is a board-certified orthopaedic spine surgeon whose extraordinary journey spans continents, cultures, and decades of medical practice excellence. Orphaned in wartime China and adopted at the age of six by Eileen and Stephen Tsou, Paul was raised with a powerful blend of Methodist Christian faith and Confucian principles. These early influences shaped a character rooted in self-reliance, ethical conviction, and deep respect for service and education, traits that remained unshakable throughout his life.

After immigrating to the United States, Paul began formal schooling in Coaldale, Pennsylvania, and went on to attend secondary schools across America, including New York City, New Mexico, and California. He studied at San Jose State College and Stanford University before earning his medical degree from the University of California, San Francisco (UCSF) School of Medicine. During the Vietnam War, he fulfilled his Selective Service obligation as a U.S. Public Health Service medical officer, serving aboard the *USCG Cutters Spencer* and *Bering Strait*.

Following his military service, Dr. Tsou completed his orthopaedic surgery residency at UCSF, where he met and married Dr. Schumarry Chao. He later pursued a prestigious spine fellowship under Professor Arthur Hodgson at the University of Hong Kong and Duchess of Kent Children's Hospital, gaining expertise in anterior spinal procedures and tuberculosis-related spinal pathology.

Dr. Tsou built a thriving private orthopaedic practice in Santa Monica, California, where he also served as a volunteer UCLA teaching assistant for over 30 years. In the final decade of his clinical career, he transitioned to a paid staff position at UCLA, attending residents and seeing patients in the university's outpatient clinics as well as performing surgeries at the UCLA Santa Monica Campus.

A published scholar, Dr. Tsou authored 20 peer-reviewed research articles, all independently or spouse-funded. About half of his peer reviewed published research papers were written during this last ten years active professional life at UCLA. He held continuous California medical licensure since 1966. He was an active member of the Scoliosis Research Society, the North American Spine Society, and served for over a decade as a California State Panel Qualified Medical Evaluator, provide the "substantial" medical evidence in resolving complex workers' compensation cases.

Now in his eighties, Dr. Tsou continues to walk two to three miles daily, reflecting on a life well lived, and remains a devoted husband, father, and a lifelong knowledge seeker.

# Autobiography Overview

### Part One: From Orphan to Medical School Graduate

Moody Tsou stepped into two different cultures during the early years of his life. He spent his first ten years immersed in Chinese traditions (1941–1951), followed by a decade of American pre-doctorate education (1951–1961), each shaping his identity.

In China, early education followed a strict tradition; children learned only Chinese, as no other language was considered appropriate. Moody (whose biological mother's family name was Lin) studied exclusively in Chinese until he was 11. At age 11 and 9 months, he immigrated to America, where his education took a new direction. He attended secondary schools in New York City, Albuquerque, NM, and Redwood City, CA. He then attended colleges in California for three years and, at 23, graduated from the University of California, San Francisco School of Medicine.

### Part Two Overview

That was the Selective Service obligation Paul agreed to, two years with the U.S. Public Health Service. Simple enough, he thought. But the fine print told a different story, including the possibility of spending months at sea aboard unpredictable, gyroting ships. Inescapable, he shipped out on one, or then added, the second U.S. Coast Guard Cutter tour.

The follow-up reward: An orthopaedic residency and a spine fellowship. And, most importantly, the greatest gift of all, God gave him Schumarry, his wife. Old friends from residency times, introduced Paul into private orthopaedic practice in Santa Monica, California.

To fulfill his Selective Service obligation, Paul served aboard two U.S. Coast Guard Cutters and worked briefly in the U.S. Public Health Service (USPHS) clinics. His service earned him Vietnam War Unit Citations.

## Part Three: Residency, Fellowship & the New Beginnings

After Paul had fulfilled his military duties, he completed an orthopaedic residency at UCSF and a spine fellowship at the University of Hong Kong.

Between these two rigorous postdoctoral training programs, Paul and Schumarry met and married. Soon after, he found an opportunity to begin his orthopaedic practice in Santa Monica. In this beach town, he worked until his retirement in 2012.

## Part Four: A Longevity of Life of Love, Marriage, and Good Health in One of America's Most Glamorous Cities

Paul and Schumarry built their lives in one of the most desirable places in America. In a place where distractions abound, long-lasting love, marriage, and good health are rare gifts. Yet, they became one of the few exceptions.

Paul met his future wife, Schumarry, on the beaches of Waikiki, Honolulu. Four months later, against her parents' wishes, they were married. She chose a plain-wrapped doctor, rather than the more polished suitors her parents had envisioned.

Starting his orthopaedic practice in Santa Monica, Paul quickly learned the role as the junior partner of the firm, He took on the most complex and challenging cases, never turning down work. He eliminated words like "frustrated," "tired," and "come back tomorrow" from his vocabulary. Despite a demanding career, he made it a priority to take as many vacations as his office partners would allow, though those breaks from work often depended on whether his children gave him the time. He ensured both of them attended the best schools, valuing their education as much as his own.

## Part Five: A Lifelong Commitment to Learning

Learn deeply. Save your friends a few dollars. Ease their health anxieties when they come to consult you with concerns.

Paul's philosophy of learning has always been immersive, whether in his profession or personal pursuits. His approach was simple: actively seek deeper knowledge, embrace the unknown, take no shortcuts before mastering the fundamentals, and acquire knowledge before technique.

Even in retirement, his broad medical and orthopaedic expertise continues to serve him. He helps friends and loved ones navigate the complexities of modern healthcare, where corporately driven checklists and AI-generated diagnoses often replace years of bedside experience.

Who is in charge here? AI algorithms have added to group consensus, which has replaced the wisdom gained from years of hands-on patient care of the individual healer. But what happens when a practitioner no longer knows how to take a proper medical history or perform a thorough physical examination?

Paul remains steadfast in his belief that real medicine is rooted in human connection, critical thinking, and a lifelong commitment to learning.

# INDEX

## D

Dai Phu Quoc Island, Vietnam

Duster, Plymouth (first car after Paul's spine fellowship, returned from HK)

## E

Echo Park, Los Angeles

Education – Secondary schools: Booker T. Washington Middle School, NYC

Highland High School, Albuquerque

Jefferson Junior High School

Sequoia High School, Redwood City

Education – Undergraduate college & Graduate & post graduate : San Jose State College

Stanford University

University of Southern California.

BS, MBA Education – Medical: St. John University of Shanghai University of California, San Francisco

University of California, Los Angeles

## F

Fellowship, Spine – University of Hong Kong

Ford Monarch (vehicle)

## G

General Medical Officer of uniformed services. (GMO) Glauber Liese, MD Chairman of Radiology at Queens Hospital

## H

H-Graft (spinal fusion technique)

Halo-pelvic distraction

Harvard Medical School

Highland High School, of Albuquerque,

Hodgeson Artur, FRCS. HK U, Professor, anterior spine surgery

Houston, TX. USPHS clinic

## I

India Reservation (USPHS a

Initial Public Offering (IPO)

Internal Medicine

Islet cell research

## J

Jefferson Junior High School
Jewelry (Burma ruby)

## K

Kerry, John (Swift Boat skipper; U.S. senator; presidential candidate)

## L

Laser used spine surgery (Holmium YAG)
Las Vegas, NV
Law Career – Lisa
Leung, John, FRCS
Lueng, Tony, MD. Laser, minimal spine surgery
Lisa Tsou
Longitudinal Rod Fixation

## M

Marital Stability
Marriage – Stanford Memorial Church
McDaniel, Dan, MD
McGonigle, John, MD
Marlborough School, Hancock Park, LA
MedImpact, a PBM
Miss Chinatown Los Angeles
Movie Script t
Murray, William, MD
Musculoskeletal Disease

## N

Nachemson, Alf, MD. Mentometer obtained disc pressure.
Nancy Swartz, MD, Paul's classmate
Neural crest (embryology)
Nung River (fictional river in film)

## O

Orthopaedic private practice
Orthopaedic trauma
Oxford University (study abroad)

# P

Palm Springs Jeweler
Panel Qualified Medical Examiner (QME)
Paul Tsou
Pelvic Pins – Halo complications
Plymouth Duster
Posterior spinal surgery
Private Practice Transition
Puogeot (French car)
Patrol Boat Swift.

# Q

Queen Mary Hospital, H. K. Queen's Hospital, Honolulu

# R

Rancho Los Amigos Hospital
Reagan, Ronald Hospital, LA
Residency Training
Rio de Janeiro (jewelry anecdote)

# S

Saint John's Hospital, Santa Monica
Sand Island, Coast Guard Base, Honolulu
Santa Monica, CA
Santa Monica Hospital
Schumarry Chao (maiden name)
Sequoia High School
Sisters of Charity
Sleep Apnea
Sonoma State Hospital
Spencer, USCG Cutter (W 36)
Spinal Canal Measurements
Spinal Deformity
Spine Fellowship
Spine Surgery Techniques
Spine Trauma
Sports Medicine
St. John's Medical School of Shanghai
Stanford Memorial Church